Buffer Annuities
No-Fee Bond-Alternatives
for a Smarter Withdrawal Strategy

Written By: **Mark J. Orr, CFP® RICP®**
Certified Financial Planner™
Retirement Income Certified Professional®

To learn more about retirement planning, go to the website below and register to join his email list.
www.SmartFinancialPlanning.com

Author of:
"Retirement Income Planning: The Baby-Boomer's 2022 Guide to Maximize Your Income and Make it Last"
"Social Security Income Planning: Baby-Boomer's Guide"
"Get Me to ZERO: 7 Tax Strategies
for a TAX-FREE Retirement"

2nd Edition -- Copyright 2022

All rights are fully reserved, and any infringements of such right will be vigorously protected/ enforced by all available legal means and financial restitution sought. This book is protected by the U.S. and International copyright laws. The reproduction, modification, distribution, transmission, republication, or display of the content in this book is strictly prohibited without prior express written permission from the Author. Any trademarked names in this book are the sole property of their respective companies.

Table of Contents

The 60%/40% Portfolio is Dead   Pg. 4
Does The 4% Rule Work?   Pg. 8
What's Sequence of Returns Risk?   Pg. 12
Hedge Funds For the Rich   Pg. 26
Buffer Annuities For the Rest of Us   Pg. 29
Vanguard's 10-Year Market Predictions   Pg. 71
RMD and Income Withdrawal Strategy   Pg. 75
About the Author   Pg. 95
Acknowledgments and Disclosures   Pg. 97

Buffer Annuities
No-Fee Bond-Alternatives
for a Smarter Withdrawal Strategy

Before we go into what Buffer annuities are (my own name for them) and why they can be instrumental in client portfolios, I'd like to begin with some background and context. As you understand the issues, it's easier to see potential solutions to income withdrawal problems.

Then we'll look at the types of investment returns Buffer annuities have returned in the past – to keep you interested. You'll be surprised. And finally, how they work.

First of all, Buffer annuities are my name for a very few and little-known annuities built for excellent growth (accumulation) without any market risk (100% principal protection) and <u>no mandatory fees/expenses</u>. And we use them as a unique buffering device when markets fall.

I'm not writing about annuities with guaranteed lifetime income. Many of my clients (as well as my wife) do have these as part of a retirement income plan (acting as a private pension). These can be a powerful addition for a growing retirement income without market risk.

But this book is going to focus on using Buffer annuities as bond alternatives to help make the 4% rule work. Why would anyone want to replace or supplement bonds in an investment portfolio? Well, let's explore the problem.

The 60%/40% Portfolio is Dead

On Nov 19, 2019, Bank of America declared 'the end of the 60/40 standard portfolio" (60% stocks and 40% fixed income/bonds). In a research note published by Bank of America Securities titled "The End of 60/40 Portfolio," strategists Derek Harris and Jared Woodard argue that "there are good reasons to reconsider the role of bonds in your portfolio."

On July 2nd, JP Morgan joined the list of Wall Street banks, calling for the demise of 60/40 portfolio despite its success this year. Their market strategists say a "traditional 60/40 portfolio will deliver annual returns of 3.5% over the next decade, compared with up to 10% over the past few decades." Those returns are not adjusted for inflation.

An article on 10/3/2020 in Barron's entitled, "A 60/40 Stocks/Bond Strategy Doesn't Work."

On 11/17/2020, CNBC interviewed Van Eck Associates CEO Jan Van Eck said, "The phrase we've been talking about with clients is 'the 40% is broken," meaning the 40% of your portfolio that's supposed to be in bonds.

An article on Bloomberg.com on 3/9/2021, stated "Two of the world's largest sovereign wealth funds say investors should expect much lower returns going forward in part because the typical balanced portfolio of 60/40 stocks and bonds no longer work as well in the current rate environment."

The article went on to say, "Thanks to declining returns from bonds, the model 60/40 portfolio may eke out real returns -- after inflation -- of just 1%-2% a year over the next decade, said Lim Chow Kiat, chief executive officer of GIC (Singapore's Sovereign Wealth Fund). That compares with gains of 6%-8% over the past 30 to 40 years, he said."

Inflation-adjusted returns average of 2% is not going to work for most American retirees. Not for a 25-30+ year retirement (a nicer way to describe being unemployed).

So what are retirees supposed to do with the 40% bond allocation? Where can they turn?

Well, before we answer that question, let's look at a more fundamental decision. What is your philosophy on retirement income planning?

Wade Pfau, Ph. D., CFA, is a Professor of Retirement Income in the Ph.D. program at the American College. He holds a doctorate in Economics from Princeton University and is well respected in the discipline of retirement income. He is the co-editor of the Journal of Personal Finance and has published many articles in financial industry journals and the Wall Street Journal, New York Times, Money Magazine, etc.

He is also a significant contributor to the RICP® designation curriculum. In his works, he often writes about two fundamentally different retirement income philosophies, which he calls: "probability-based" and "safety first."

Each one has its pros and cons. Primarily choosing one belief over the other will set the overall direction and predictability of lifestyle of one's future income.

Those favoring "probability-based" will believe that the markets will provide large enough returns over time to compensate for the occasional yet likely negative returns. They say, "why should they give up the upside?" in return for lower returns with more guarantees?

-40% or less	-40% to -30%	-30% to -20%	-20% to -10%	-10% to 0%	0% to 10%	10% to 20%	20% to 30%	30% to 40%	40% or more
						1993			
						2004			
						1968			
						1926			
						2016			
						1959			
						1985			
						2014		1982	
					1960	1971	1999	1991	
				2000	1994	2010	2017	1950	
				1962	2015	2006	1983	2019	
				1932	2011	2012	1963	1985	
				1946	1970	1964	1996	1989	
				1929	2005	1988	1951	1980	
				1969	1947	2020	1967	1936	
				1977	2007	1952	1976	2013	
			1973	1981	1948	1949	1943	1955	
			1941	2018	1987	1986	2009	1997	1958
			2001	1990	1984	1979	1961	1945	1928
		1974	1940	1953	1978	1972	1998	1975	1935
	2008	1930	1957	1934	1956	1944	2003	1995	1933
1931	1937	2002	1966	1939	1992	1942	1938	1927	1954

PROACTIVE ✓
Tax Planning

Yes, the Probability-based crowd can rightfully say that stocks have returned about 10% a year over the last 100 or so years. But as anyone can plainly see, those annual returns are all over the place – and very random.

But their opponents point out that this philosophy leaves folks with both market risk (sequence of returns discussed in a moment) and longevity risk. This might mean outliving one's money and cutting lifestyle.

Although this book primarily teaches how to take some bond risk off of your table – that the S&P 500 bell curve chart above shows that most will already be taking plenty of risk with the equities in their portfolio.

The "safety-first" mindset believes that at least the essential costs of living expenses should be covered by guaranteed income from Social Security, pensions, and fixed income annuities. These income sources are guaranteed and the risk of living too long and outliving your money.

Lifestyle expenses "above" your monthly necessities and leaving a legacy could be met by using market-based investments. They believe this is more prudent.

You might remember the "what's your number?" commercials on TV. You know, the ones that had people carrying around big orange numbers that they thought was the amount of money they would need to retire. In other words, their retirement savings goal.

What number did you think "your number" was? Did you have any idea where to start making your number goal? Is it $350,000? $1,000,000? $2,500,000?

The 4% Rule

Well, maybe you saw an article in Money Magazine years ago that talked about the "4% rule." It's the Suzy Orman and many other so-called sages "rule of thumb" for retirement income planning.

Here's what it is (or was) all about. In 1994, financial planner William Bengen developed the 4% rule. It quickly became the guiding "formula" used by professional advisors and do-it-yourselfers for about two decades.

The 4% rule (or theory) says that at retirement, with a portfolio of 60% stocks and 40% bonds, one could withdraw 4% of the initial savings (and increase it by inflation every year). Then the retiree would have a 90% chance of his income continuing for 30 years without the savings being completely depleted until the end of those 30 years.

By the way, a 100% stock or a 100% bond portfolio has less than a 60% chance of lasting 30 years. Under most long-term market scenarios (back-testing), a 60%/40% worked the best.

So, for example, someone with $1 million at retirement could withdraw $40,000 in the first year. If inflation was 3% that year, the second year, they could withdraw $41,200. That growing income could conceivably last for 30 years until the savings and income stream would be all gone.

Of course, it's even possible that your account could be much larger at the end of 30 years. Or it may not last at all.

The 4% (and similar rules) fall under Dr. Pfau's "probability-based" income philosophy rather than the "safety-first" approach.

Have you already decided which mindset you favor? If you got on a plane and the pilot announced the "good news" is that there is a 90% chance of landing safely at your destination, would you get off that plane? I would!

The stock markets are at all-time highs now. And then there's the upcoming end to the 30-year long bull market in bonds (if you believe that interest rates will rise to more normal levels as investors will demand higher returns from riskier borrowers as government, corporate, and all other types of debt continues to skyrocket). Do you believe that a 90% chance is optimistic now? Who knows?

Mr. Bengen understands that as interest rates rise, the value of bonds will drop. This makes a diversified portfolio of even 30%-40% bonds riskier now. The other reason this theory is not blindly used nearly as much anymore is largely due to something called the "sequence of returns" risk.

I'll be writing a lot about this investment risk in the pages that follow. In broad terms, the sequence of returns risk is stock losses early in your retirement can have a major effect on whether you outlive your money or not.

But for now, I'll leave it at that. Morningstar has since (2013) come out with its 2.8% rule (replacing the more aggressive 4% rule), saying that it is a safer withdrawal rate than a 60%/40% (stock/bond) portfolio could reasonably rely on for a 30-year retirement.

That means that $1,000,000 retiree could withdraw $28,000 their first year in retirement and have that figure grow by inflation.

An article in the Wall Street Journal in March 2013 entitled "Say Goodbye to The 4% Rule," suggested a 2% initial withdrawal rate would more safely (with a much higher probability) bring someone successfully through a 30-year retirement.

The article states: "If you had retired Jan. 1, 2000, with an initial 4% withdrawal rate and a portfolio of 55% stocks and 45% bonds rebalanced each month, with the first year's withdrawal amount increased by 3% a year for inflation, your portfolio would have fallen by a third through 2010, according to investment firm T. Rowe Price Group. And you would be left with only a 29% chance of making it through three decades, the firm estimates."

The last sentence is the real potential warning. My next question, is what if you (or your spouse) live longer than 30 years in retirement? We are retiring earlier and living longer! It's a strong possibility for many folks as longevity is by far the largest of the risks in retirement.

These "rules" ignore an income need over a longer potential retirement for you and/or your spouse.

Some academics say that the safe withdrawal figure for a 40-year retirement plan is now only 1.5%, according to some new academic research. Personally, I cannot wrap my head around this low of a figure, but I do agree the "safe" withdrawal rate for 35-40 years must be lower than one for a 30-year retirement. That's just plain common sense.

Now many folks believe there is no way that they will live 30 years in retirement. But I'll remind you that if a couple has made it to age 65, there is a 50% probability that at least one of them will live to age 92. And a 25% chance at least one of them will celebrate their age 95th birthday (and perhaps more). Those statistics are actuarial facts.

And for better educated, wealthier, and healthier retirees, the odds of living longer than that are even better.

The strides being made every year in medical science are well-known. Cancer could be cured, heart attacks avoided. We can only hope.

In any case, would you rather plan on a 20-year retirement and be out of luck if you (or your spouse) live 25 years… or plan on a 35-year retirement income stream and only live 25 years? Unless you or your spouse's health is not good, I hope that the answer is self-evident.

Many investors have a hard time understanding that if their portfolio earns 4%, and they take out 4% every year for living expenses, why would their principal go down. Shouldn't it stay level forever?

The problem with that logic is that it fails to take inflation into account. If your expenses are going up by 2%-3% a year, then your portfolio would have to gain that much each year on top of the 4% you take out.

And over time, the bite of inflation is harsh. At just 3% inflation, your monthly expenses will have doubled in about 24 years – from the start of your retirement until you or your spouse are well into your golden years.

It also fails to account for the potential of rising taxes. If taxes go up, you'll need to withdraw more money out of your accounts just to live the same lifestyle.

Ok, now let's add the biggest wrinkle to the 4% rule – the Sequence of Returns Risk.

Sequence of Returns Risk

This is how the mutual fund company Thornburg Investment Management defines sequence of return risk: "Sequence of returns is simply the order in which returns are realized by a retiree. The consequences of a bad sequence of returns, especially early in retirement, can mean a premature depletion of the portfolio. Retirees need to avoid being in the position of having to sell during inopportune market environments."

I'll add more practical value and an eye-opening example next.

Given the heights of the market now, it should be a warning. Rob Williams, managing director of income planning at the Schwab Center for Financial Research says: "When you're withdrawing funds at the same time that your portfolio is losing value, you can expose yourself to a phenomenon known as sequence-of-returns risk.

The order in which investment returns occur can have a huge impact on your assets' long-term if you are taking withdrawals from (or even adding to) your portfolio."

The biggest risk is during the withdrawal phase. Let me be clear that the sequence of returns risk does not apply to a lump sum of assets.

The risk is only dangerous while taking an income stream from your savings – particularly when the investment returns early in your retirement are hugely negative or very poor.

You've heard the expression "timing is everything." Well, your Sequence of Returns could work for you... or against you in taking income from your investments, as you'll see.

Here's an example of how a poor sequence of returns can destroy a long-term retirement plan.

And just for "old-times" sake, I'll also use a 5% withdrawal rate in the example too (so many people think that if my portfolio averages 7% then, taking a 5% withdrawal rate should leave me with a larger balance than I started with 30 years from now!).

That's not correct as it ignores the compounding effect of inflation – which can be a powerful headwind against a successful retirement.

Let's look at actual returns of the S&P 500 index (with no fees or taxes) from 1989 to 2008. Then let's take those same exact returns and reverse the order they came in (2008-1989). You'll notice that both sequences have the exact same average return of 8.49% (typo in the chart).

There is no difference in the average rate of return -- if withdrawals are not being taken. The sequence of returns has no effect on a lump sum with no withdrawals.

The middle column is the actual price returns of the S&P 500 from 1989 to 2008. The column on the far right is the same exact index returns... but in reverse order (2008 back to 1989). The same index, just a different order of returns.

So, if we have a hypothetical account valued at $1,000,000 and we withdraw $50,000 (5%) and adjust that for inflation (we'll use a 3% constant inflation rate for all years), let's see how the two sequences of returns (the actual S&P 500 index returns plus the same returns in the reverse order) plays out.

Year	1989-2008 Sequence	2008-1989 Sequence
1	31.69%	-37.00%
2	-3.11%	5.49%
3	30.47%	15.84%
4	7.62%	4.91%
5	10.08%	10.88%
6	1.32%	28.68%
7	37.58%	-22.10%
8	22.96%	-11.88%
9	33.36%	-9.11%
10	28.58%	21.04%
11	21.04%	28.58%
12	-9.11%	33.36%
13	-11.88%	22.96%
14	-22.10%	37.58%
15	28.68%	1.32%
16	10.88%	10.08%
17	4.91%	7.62%
18	15.84%	30.47%
19	5.49%	-3.11%
20	-37.00%	31.69%
AVG.	8.43%	8.49%

Withdrawals start at $50,000/ year and rise to $90,000 annually over the two decades (to combat inflation). After only 20 years in retirement, the 1989–2008 sequence has more than supported the retirement spending and even allowed the account value to grow to over $3.1 million. The early years of good returns made this possible. The big losses came in the second half of the two decades. In this example, the "probability-based" model worked out absolutely perfectly.

Continuing to take out $90,000 plus 3% inflation withdrawals is not going to pose a problem at all for a 30+ year retirement. But this is not a typical bull market. I certainly would not want to plan my own retirement income stream on a possible 20-year bull market.

Again, "timing is everything." Timing and the "probability-based" model could work well for you and dramatically increase your savings... or against you in taking income from your investments, so you outlive your savings.

And the differences could be very dramatic, with wide swings in possible outcomes. However, the results for the 2008–1989 sequence (reverse order) are very different, with the heavy losses coming in the first half of the period.

The first-year loss of -37%, which was followed by significant negative returns (three years in a row) in years 7, 8, and 9 dramatically reduced the total account value to only about $235,000 at the end of the 20 years.

With an account balance of just $235,000 at the end of 20 years, there is virtually no way that anyone could take out $90,000 a year at that point and last more than three years before the account would run dry.

In this case, the "probability-based" philosophy would not have worked out so well. In fact, it would have been a disastrous outcome for a 30-year retirement.

So, the sequence of returns while taking income withdrawals had a huge swing in potential outcomes.

I can also show you actual annual returns when the S&P 500 averaged 9% a year – with only a 4% withdrawal rate (the 4% rule) and the portfolio blew up. Out of money!

On the rosy side, the account more than tripled – despite taking substantial income along the way. On the opposite end of the spectrum – with a bad sequence of returns, the account diminished by 73% and had no realistic shot of providing even a 24-year income to the retiree.

The range of possible retirement income risks and outcomes is probably wider than it's ever been with the globalization of our economy. We could see high stock returns, big negative stock returns, high inflation, deflation, higher taxes, and more changes in government policy (Social Security, Medicare, etc.).

Buffer annuities can help retirees lessen the pain of the sequence of returns risk and perhaps virtually eliminate this huge risk to your retirement savings – whether taking Requited Minimum Distributions (RMDs) or just taking withdrawals to meet your living expenses.

We'll delve into the above more a bit later on.

Financial advisors David Gaylor and his partner Gary Reed are two of my friends and mentors are as well. David writes a story in his book that we use in our educational classes teaching retirement income planning to pre-retirees. I'm going to pass it along to my readers here – giving full credit where it's due!

It's the story of brother and sister, Bill and Jill, who are three years apart in age. But all other circumstances they share are identical. The only difference is, "Jill was born three years too late!"

You see, Bill retired with $1,000,000 in 1996, and Jill retired three years later in 1999. Jill had an equal amount of savings as her older brother at her retirement. Only the "sequence of returns risk" is shown here – no other potential risks are factored in.

Both had heard on the radio that they should only invest in low-cost index funds (to pay virtually no fees). They were both excited about the big returns in the US stock market. In the late 1990s, everyone was making money.

In fact, the indexes were lagging most of the companies in the tech sector, but they liked the idea of diversification at a low cost. Set it and forget it!

When Bill retired in 1996, he began using the 4% rule, which had really become popular in the 1990s and was talked about on the radio and in magazines as a "safe" way of not running out of money for 30 years.

So, Bill started taking income of $40,000 and increased his withdrawals by a 3% constant inflation rate each year to keep his purchasing power equal to inflation.

Bill retired at an excellent time. He had very good returns in 1996, 1997, 1998, and 1999. Yes, he suffered like most everyone else in 2000-2002.

But starting with those first four years, and even taking into account seven years of increasing withdrawals, his account never dipped below $1,000,000. And during the recovery of 2003-2007, his account actually grew to nearly $1.5 million – while continuing to take income that had grown to over $55,000 a year.

Despite his income growing to about $68,000 in 2014 and suffering through the 2007-2009 bear market (the worst since the depression), his account was still worth nearly $1.5 million. Bill took out over $1,004,000 in withdrawals over those 19 years, and his account actually grew by +49% on top of that!

The sequence of returns happened to be on "his side." Of course, it was just luck. No skill or advanced planning. Bill ended up in great shape for the next 10, 15, or even 20 years. He will have no income worries and have real peace of mind. And he'll be able to leave a nice legacy for his children, grandkids, and/or charity.

"Probability-based" planning worked well in this case. But the timing of his retirement was purely by chance!

Now let's look at what happened to his younger sister Jill. Retiring with the same one million dollars – but her retirement picture would look very different only three years later. She used the same 4% rule as Bill and the same low-cost index funds. But the timing of her retirement was not very good.

As you'll see, the randomness of the sequence of returns was not on "her side" when she started taking income in Jan. 1999 – even though the index returned +8.91% that first year. She would have been better off with "safety-first" thinking. Losses in 2000, 2001, 2002, and then a whopping loss in 2008 ruined the long-term health of her retirement.

Those investment losses, along with her $40,000 and growing distributions, caused her account value to drop to just over $316,000 -- just ten years into her retirement!

That's a -68% reduction from her initial one million dollars of savings. Even though 2008 was the last year that she suffered a loss, by continuing those growing withdrawals, her account was only valued at $283,000 by the end of 2014 – just 16 years into her retirement!

With 2015 being a very "flat" year in the index, her withdrawal of about $64,000 in that year would have left her account valued at some $220,000.

She "might" have only four or five years left of income before her savings are all gone.

Now Bill and Jill's story only focuses on the sequence of returns. No changes in tax rates, inflation, health care costs, or public policy. The longer one lives the larger those other risks become.

About a dozen years ago, a "brand-name" insurance company started teaching both advisors and consumers about something they called the "Retirement Red Zone."

They defined the retirement red zone as the five years right before you retire and the first five years of being retired. They promoted it pretty heavily, and it makes perfect sense and is completely in line with the reality of the sequence of returns risk.

But as we saw with Jill – those first ten years killed her "dream" retirement income plan. I like to alter the "red zone" definition to cover 15 years, to the five years before retirement and the first TEN years of "unemployment!"

Are you a football fan? If so, you've heard the TV commentators talk about the "red zone" as the area within 20 yards of the goal line. The offense may have driven the ball all the way down the field and gotten close to scoring a touchdown. But defenses get stronger in the red zone as there is less field to defend. It's harder to score in the red zone.

The NFL even has a statistic called "red zone efficiency." It is the percentage of the time an offense scores a TD when they made it to the red zone.

What does football have to do with retirement?

Well, think of moving the football down the field as accumulating retirement savings. Then you get to the retirement red zone – the most critical time in retirement.

It's the hardest part to navigate and successfully "score" (being Bill rather than Jill). And that huge insurance company was only referring to risks of investment returns during those years – but makes no mention of the other risks to retirement (mentioned above).

The "probability-based" folks focus on the 90% chance of retirement success, while those identifying with the "safety-first" philosophy focus more on the 10% chance of retirement failure – outliving your money.

I believe in "safety-first" planning for your basic and essential expenses. Using the "probability-based" (getting both market risks and rewards) for fun spending and legacy with much less stress! Our firm does this very well.

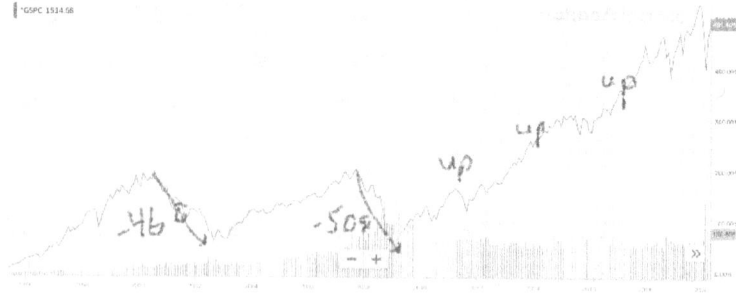

As I began writing this book section, the stock market (S&P 500 index) has hit a new all-time high in June 2021.

Look at this chart above, which shows the S&P 500 index from 1996 through Dec 2020. All-time record highs during a pandemic! New highs again in late 2021! The result of the Fed Gov. spending TRILLIONs of borrowed dollars.

What do you see in the future – a situation more like Bill's or Jill's? Are you in the retirement red zone? After looking at this chart, my next question is, where do you think the index is more likely to head in the next few years – continue going way up... or retrace some of its huge gains for a bit?

Or maybe head toward the lows of 2008 and 2009? Is this an ideal time to rely on a "probability-based" retirement plan? Is the likelihood better for +25% up or -25% down?

U.S. corporate profit growth (which smart accountants can make whatever they want them to be) has been slowing. Sales are not really growing either. There are many stock market indicators that point to another market "event." But with bond interest rates so low around the world, the market is not slowing down.

Over the last eleven years, the rise in stock prices has had more to do with Fed actions, company stock buybacks (with borrowed money), greed, and extremely low interest-paying investment alternatives than a huge profit outlook for corporate America.

Price/Earnings ratios are pretty high. Anyway, for a "probability-based" investor retiring in the near future, the chart shows pretty clearly that the sequence of return risk -- is probably not going to be their friend at this point in time.

Always keep in mind that if you lose -35% -- you need +53.8% returns... just to get back to even.

Percent Loss	Percent Gain
5%	5.3%
10%	11.1%
15%	17.6%
20%	25.0%
25%	33.3%
30%	42.9%
35%	53.8%
40%	66.7%
45%	81.8%
50%	100.0%

And it's not only stocks that can lose money. Bonds can lose value too. Even bonds that the US government guarantees can lose money (if sold before maturity).

Update: I just posted the following graph on LinkedIn today with an. Pretty interesting.

The Bloomberg Barclays U.S. Long Term Treasury Total

Return Index is currently experiencing its most significant drawdown (loss of value) to date. It's plummeted more than 20% as Long-Term Treasuries continue to sell off amidst skyrocketing inflation expectations, lifting the U.S. 10-Year Treasury Yield to 1.75%.

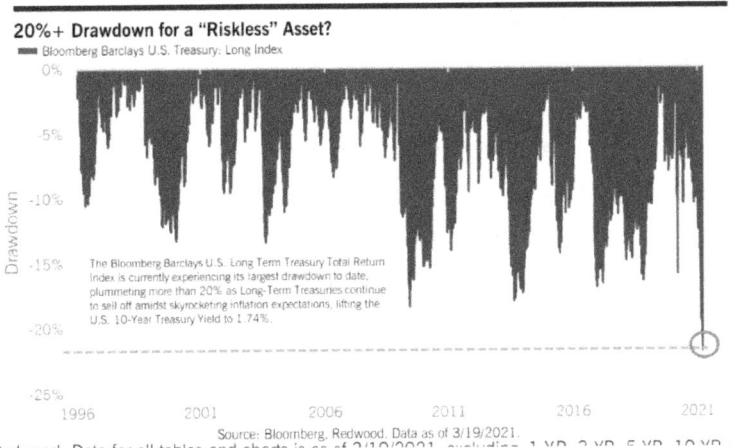

A 20% drop in value for what is thought to be the safest investment in the world! More clear and compelling evidence that bonds should not be as prevalent in portfolios right now and bond alternatives should be fully explored!

And you are in the right place to do so. What's the answer for somebody planning on retiring in the next 1-5 years? Or are you already in the first 5-10 years of retirement?

I run my retirement "safety-first" practice under the guidance of the four "S's": Smart, Secure, Simple, and Solutions.

Smart means that you don't take ANY more risk than you need to achieve your monthly income and legacy goals.

Is there really any potential return worth losing sleep over and putting much of your life savings at risk? Is it 11%, 16% or 20%? How much risk are you willing to take? How much risk can you afford to take? How much total risk do you want to take?

Secure means thinking more about your downside protection than a potential upside gain. Consider the "What IF you're wrong?" scenario on any number of life's unforeseen events (retirement risks).

Simple. People must understand their plan and why they are taking any particular step. It has to be 100% transparent too.

And finally, **Solutions.** Retirement planning is much more about "planning" than "products." Products just fill the need. So, planning solutions (financial products and services) must encompass the other three S's. Does your retirement planning strategy comply with the four S's at this point?

Ok, I'm sure you think I've beat "the sequence of returns risk" to death. And you might be correct, but this is a huge risk to a successful retirement (not running out of money). We're almost ready to get into the subject at hand – Buffer annuities. Or what I also call the "Poor Man's Hedge Fund." How familiar are you with hedge funds?

Hedge Funds

Of course, Buffer annuities are not hedge funds at all. Hedge funds are typically open only to Accredited Investors (who are worth $1 million or more – exclusive of their primary home or have an income of at least $200,000 (single) or $300,000 married for the last 2 years.

Lots of folks can meet that requirement. Although many still are, a good number of hedge funds have marketed themselves as superior long-term investments (over the S&P 500). A few have actually achieved that goal – but thousands of them have gone out of business too.

In times of market volatility, hedge funds attract billions of dollars – even though many underperform the S&P 500 index over 3, 5, or 10 years. Hedge funds managers generally charge 2% annual management fees plus 20% of your profits (you take ALL the risk since they do not share or participate in any of your losses!)

Hedge funds usually have a $250,000+ min investment. The better ones have a $1,000,000 minimum, while others have a $5,000,000 or larger minimum.

And your money is typically tied up in the fund for 5, 7, or 10 years before you can get it all out. Not happy – well, you're pretty much stuck!

So if you put $1,000,000 into a hedge fund with a 2% annual fee, the manager gets $20,000 per year.

And if the manager makes intelligent investment decisions (or gets lucky), and he makes a $300,000 profit on your investment – they get an additional $60,000 in profit sharing.

Wouldn't that be so fun to brag about at a cocktail party or on the golf course that you invested in XYZ Hedge Fund with a 30% gain?

So now you have $1,220,000 ($1,000,000 + $300,000 gain minus $20,000 fees and $60,000 profit share) working for you the following year. The hedge fund manager got about 26% of your profits -- while you took all of the risks!

Of course, if the fund manager losses $300,000 – you take the total loss. They still get paid their annual fee of $24,400. So now you are down $324,400 that year. Ouch!

Naturally, there are some superstar hedge funds. But the trouble is, you don't know which ones (out of literally 1,000's) the top 20 hedge funds will eventually be. They have high costs, long-term commitments, substantial risks, and no guarantees whatsoever. They are not for me!

And to get in with a great fund, you probably have to know somebody in the "boys club." Not so with Buffer annuities.

So let's get into what Buffer annuities are and give you some examples of their returns over the last 10-20 years.

They certainly aren't your father's annuities!

Buffer Annuities

I think we'll start this section off with the more exciting parts – the returns of Buffer annuities without taking any stock market risk.

Then I'll describe how they fit into my Requited Minimum Distribution (RMD) strategy to help make the 4% rule actually work in your retirement. And maybe, just maybe stretch that often disputed 4% rule to something closer to 5% or better, so you can really enjoy your retirement.

Then, I'll explain the nuts and bolts of these annuities, so you fully understand them.

In summary, you'll see what you might expect over the next 10-15 years in returns (based on the last 20 years). Then you'll see how they might fit into your retirement income strategy (the same ones I use for my clients). And finally, you'll understand precisely how they work.

First of all, unlike the high minimum investments and financial qualifications of hedge funds, Buffer annuities are really for regular folks. Most have a $20,000 minimum investment ($25K in TEXAS). The one that I like best has a minimum investment of $75,000.

I have many clients who have put $200,000 to $500,000 into their Buffer annuities. Others have invested over $1,000,000 – they understand and like them.

And some clients use other investments altogether.

When we invest a lot of money in Buffer annuities, I usually prefer to diversify between two of them, just like you would do with your portfolio. I like to do that because each Buffer annuity uses different underlying indexes. I like diversification.

The maximum investment per Buffer annuity is actually $1 million. Although if we beg, we might be able to invest a bit more.

In this, what I call a "bond hedge fund alternative," your worst return in any year is guaranteed to be zero. Not much less than bank CDs today! You take NO market risk.

There are over 120 insurance companies that are selling some 900 different annuity products. Those 900 other annuities come in all shapes, sizes, and colors.

Some are awful, some are good, and a few dozen are really worth looking at. Some are very expensive while others have no costs – just like a CD from a bank.

Some have a specific purpose and do well at serving that purpose. Others are financial "swiss army knives" that do a lot of things for you, but none particularly well.

But so far, I've found just THREE of them that truly qualify for what I call the "poor man's bond hedge fund." Three specific annuities are built for attractive accumulation potential and have NO stock market risk or any mandatory annual fees/expenses.

But, they each include something that few annuities offer, which is exceptional. You'll see as you read further that 8% average annual returns are possible (with no negative market years ever). They might provide more equity-like returns than a bond alternative!

And unlike hedge funds, all annuities are tax-deferred. You do not get any 1099 forms or pay any taxes on gains – until you take money out. You can fund them with IRA-type money or non-qualified money (non-retirement plan-type money). NO taxes are owed while interest remains inside the annuity due to the tax deferral.

There are NO FEES at all either - (unless you opt to pay a small fee for the potential to earn 8% to 15% or more in good years with no market risk) and there's no there's a cap on your potential gains or earnings either.

NO 2% hedge fund annual fees (that they charge even if your account plummets) and NO 20% profit sharing like hedge funds charge when you have a good year.

The small optional fee (it's up to you if and when to pay it) gives you the potential to earn better returns without any market risk. This feature is what separates these three annuities from the pack of Fixed Indexed Annuities.

Buffer annuities provide more upside returns but have NO income riders or phantom benefit values (which determine a guaranteed lifetime income). No death benefit riders – the death benefit is the account value, just like a CD.

You'll see sample returns over the past 10-20 years using indexes following "rules-based algorithms" in a moment.

I use 2-3 indexes in one Buffer annuity, including one managed by Fidelity and a few "offshoots" of the S&P 500 index. Again, you can never experience a market loss.

I'm using this "financial tool" for a bond fund/CD alternative since bonds/CDs are paying historically low rates and aren't likely to hit the above-cited potential returns any time soon. But folks who are wary of the lofty stock market valuations and volatility are interested too.

Again, in this fixed income hedge fund alternative. Your worst return is zero. There are no fees (unless you opt for some), only a seven or 10-year holding period. And you can get 10% of your initial investment out every single year without a penalty or any charges.

For the right people/situation, your investment funds can come from an IRA, old 401K... or non-IRA type accts (non-qualified brokerage accts, CD replacements, other annuities, etc.).

This can fit well many retirement plans. In fact, it is really best for long-term retirement money. It can be a regular IRA or, perhaps even better yet... a ROTH IRA.

And although you can earn stock-like average returns, I use these products as BOND ALTERNATIVES. And yes, there are bond alternative hedge funds as well (and real estate funds, options funds, long/short funds, etc.).

Dr. Wade Pfau, CFA, told Forbes magazine in 2015 that "bonds don't belong in a retirement portfolio." And that was when interest rates were 2-3 times higher than today! He still believes and teaches that to advisors today.

Here's the case against bonds in the traditional 60/40 portfolio. Dr. Pfau says that with the current low-interest rates of virtually all bonds and the credit risks of all non-US Treasuries plus interest rate risk for all bonds – bonds should play no more than a minor role in a retirement portfolio.

Oh yeah – and bonds have inflation risk too. A fixed coupon rate is <u>fixed</u> and has no protection against rising prices.

The argument against bonds is still happening. Warren Buffett was none too kind to bonds either in his annual shareholder letter of February 2021, where he wrote:

"And bonds are not the place to be these days. Can you believe that the income recently available from a 10-year U.S. Treasury bond – the yield was 0.93% at yearend – had fallen 94% from the 15.8% yield available in September 1981? In certain large and important countries, such as Germany and Japan, investors earn a negative return on trillions of dollars of sovereign debt. Fixed-income investors worldwide – whether pension funds, insurance companies or retirees – face a bleak future."

That's what Warren Buffett thinks.

I mostly agree with each of them – that with the current low-interest rates of virtually all bonds and the credit risks of non-US Treasuries plus interest rate risk for all bonds – bonds should play no more than a minor role in a retirement portfolio. We need to find more attractive alternatives.

I position this product as a bond fund alternative rather than competing with risky stocks, equity mutual funds, and ETFs. And maybe, as you'll see in a moment – you might need a "hedge" for stocks from now on too -- with such high CAPE ratios (explained in a moment).

But before we get into my hedge fund alternative, let me show you why so many financial professionals (including yours truly) are so concerned about bonds right now.

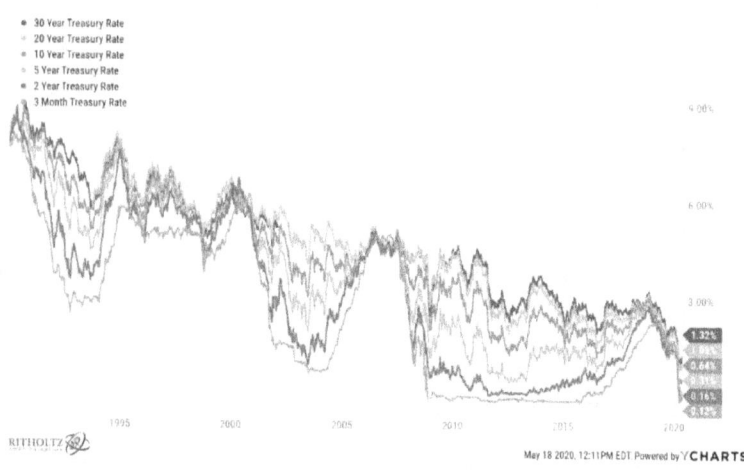

When you study the preceding chart – you'll see why we need to find more attractive bond alternatives.

In early 2021, the 10-year U.S. Treasury note yield stood at 0.68%, while the 30-year Treasury had a yield of 1.5%. In Feb 2022, the yields are 2% and 2.3%, respectively. Would you loan money to anyone at 1.4% for 30 years? Heck no.

The U.S. Aggregate Bond Index (AGG) is comprised of government debt, mortgage-backed debt, and highly rated corporate bonds offer a yield of about 2.35% today That is less than today's inflation rate of 7% (before taxes).

Keep in mind that bond coupon rates are fixed. If you buy a $100,000 of an AAA-rated 20-year corporate bond today with a fixed coupon rate of 2.5%, you'll get paid $2,500 interest every year for 20 years and then (hopefully – if you didn't buy a bond from a future Enron, etc.) you'll get your $100,000 back.

What investor can live on a fixed 2.5% income? Inflation is not fixed – it compounds over time! Even at 2% inflation, in just five years, that $2,500 of fixed income would only buy $2,260 worth of "stuff" in today's dollars. And only $2,043 worth of stuff in 10 years.

Inflation is a fixed-income investor's worst enemy. That's a loser's game long-term. Don't be a sucker.

And yes, you have credit risk with most bonds too. Although defaults are historically low, not every bond will be paid back in full.

But it gets worse. Bond prices move in the opposite direction of yields. With rising interest rates, the Barclays Bond Index has lost -3.45% so far (as of 2/11/2022).

At these historic low-interest rates, should interest rates return to more normal levels, the prices of the bonds in your portfolio will nosedive.

Now let's look at the CAPE ratio and why it may not be the best time to buy stocks, either. Yes, maybe we need a hedge fund alternative for equities as well??

CAPE Ratio vs. S&P 500

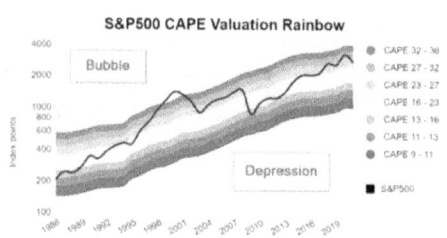

In 1999: Thanks to the tech bubble, CAPE was literally off the charts and well above twice its long-run average. Five to ten-year returns from this point were terrible, as expected.

In 2009: CAPE was pretty-cheap thanks to the financial crisis. Five to ten-year returns from this point were very good, also as expected.

End 2019: CAPE was bordering on very high (about 29) at around 75% above average. Five to ten-year returns from this point are, based in history, expected to be poor.

No matter what you think about the prospects for the stock market over the next 6-18 months, Nobel-prize winner Robert Shiller had regarded (even before COVID-19) that the stock market was overvalued, according to his famous CAPE Ratio. It's been the trillions of dollars of government spending (with borrowed dollars) that's kept the market from crashing, don't you think?

The CAPE ratio is the Cyclically Adjusted Price to Earnings ratio. Personally, I think the market had been overvalued during most of 2019 when the market went up by 30%, but real corporate earnings/cash flow/dividend increases didn't merit those high returns.

In my opinion, the rise was all about 1) the Fed printing TRILLIONS of dollars, 2) corporate stock buybacks, 3) extremely low-interest rates, 4) the public's FOMO (Fear Of Missing Out), and 5) TINA (There Is No Alternative).

You can see the BLACK line is the S&P 500. The REDDER the wavey bands are, the less likely future returns in the stock market will be even average (let alone double-digit). The more the S&P (BLACK line) is in the green/yellow bands, the better the expected returns are over the next 5-10 years. The notes on the right of the bands explain it pretty well.

As of February 2022, the CAPE ratio is 37.76. That is 92% above the modern-era market average of 19.6. That puts the current P/E over one standard deviation above the average.

This indicates that the market is Overvalued. BUT… that doesn't mean it won't keep going up for a while though. And the markets are even higher today!

Let's look at CAPE another way. The chart below shows the lower the CAPE ratio (left columns), the higher the expected returns should be over the next ten years.

Conversely, the higher the CAPE, the lower the returns are expected for the following decade.

You can see where the CAPE is (37.76) in Feb 2022. If the CAPE goes a bit higher, we should expect to see negative returns over the next ten years.

Would you want to retire under this scenario? Isn't this similar to Jill's retirement several pages back?

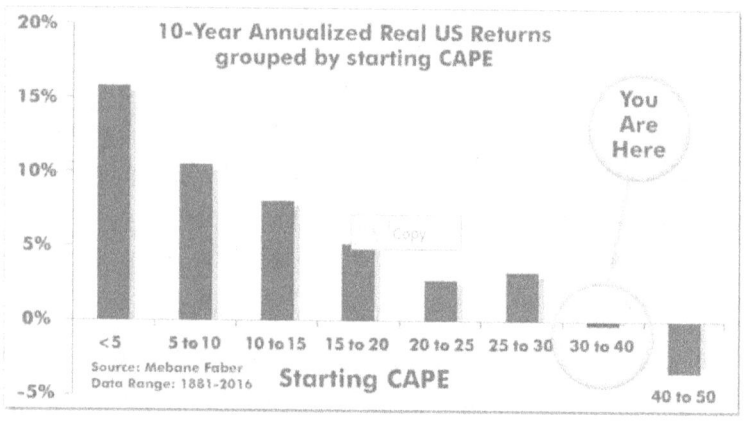

Are you still skeptical?

Let's look at a much longer history of the CAPE and future returns, OK? How about the last 121 years.

You can see that every time the CAPE was high; the returns were low in the following years. And when the CAPE was low, the returns were up like a hockey stick.

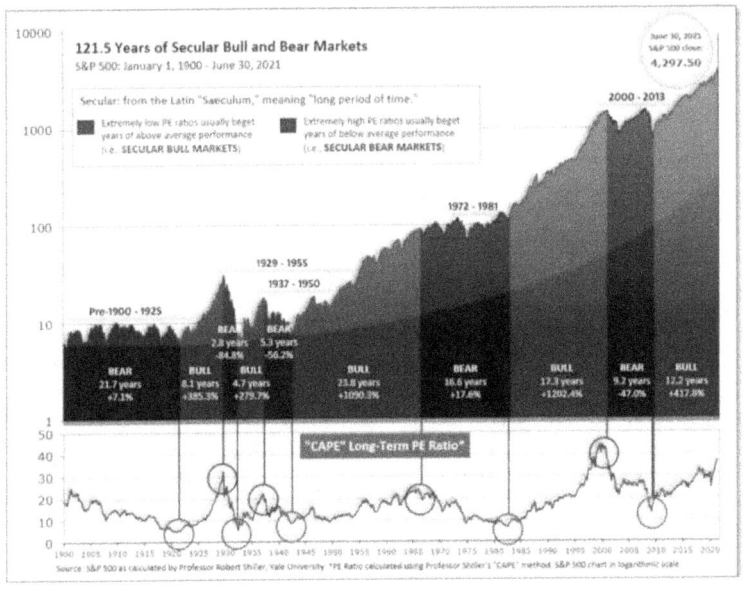

By the way, the "Buffett Indicator Model" (named after Warren Buffett (who claims this is his favorite macroeconomic indicator), is the total US stock market valuation ratio compared to GDP.

This ratio is currently 61% higher than its historical average, indicating the market is Strongly Overvalued. Of course, Buffett is not panicking… but he isn't taking withdrawals from an IRA to meet his monthly expenses either.

The stock market is going to do what it is going to do. It is often irrational and way overshoots to the upside as well, as overshoots on the downside. The market is fueled and propelled mainly by fear and greed.

Now, my clients will tell you that I'm much more of an overall strategy and planning guy... rather than a product guy.

Financial products are just financial tools – like golf clubs. They just get you around the golf course.

But these unique Buffer annuities can be an opportunity or a solution for several problems since they carry no market risk, enjoy tax-deferral (no 1099's unless you make a withdrawal of earnings), only require a medium-term commitment, and have good liquidity. Oh, and they offer some exciting potential returns too.

Your investment is backed by an A+ rated (AM BEST) insurance company. And again, your money is never invested in the markets – so your investment is never subject to market risk.

Your actual returns are simply "linked" to the returns of the indexes used. The insurer uses options on one and 2-year indexes to get returns. There are five indexes, but I typically would only use three of them, all of them diversified in the 1-year and 2-year indexes.

These three little-known products are strictly designed for tax-deferred accumulation and growth without market risk.

But I take that one step further and use them for my RMD and withdrawal strategies – so my clients don't end up like Jill. We want the 4% rule to actually work!

There are NO attractive guaranteed lifetime income options, nor any "maybe" LTC benefit "doublers" that some other annuities may offer, however much less accumulation potential.

Buffer annuities can be passive "set-it-and-forget" or actively managed once a year (which is what I suggest).

Before we look at some past returns and how flexible these three special annuities are, let's take a quick look at the broad category of annuities, OK?

You've probably seen the TV and magazine ads from the guy who "hates annuities... and thinks you should too." He owns one of the biggest investment advisory firms in the country and is worth $6.4 BILLION (Forbes Richest 400 List #151 on 2021 list). Like me, he is a financial fiduciary.

His commercials say that he "would rather die and go to hell than sell an annuity" and "I'll never sell an annuity." He's mostly talking about very high-cost variable annuities sold by many stockbrokers. I wouldn't sell one of those now either – except for maybe two very low-cost ones!

He and his multi-millionaire clients don't need annuity income to pay their monthly expenses. He could lose 95% of all of his assets in the stock market and still be very wealthy.

With his wealth, he doesn't have longevity risk either. He could live to be age 650 and never run out of money.

His financial position is very different from mine and yours.

There is one other reason why he hates annuities. He doesn't get paid on them. His fee-only firm charges his clients a fee based on the amount of money his firm manages for the client.

It's a fee for "assets under management" (AUM) arrangement.

In fact, he makes so much profit in quarterly fees, he'll even pay any surrender charges or early withdrawal penalties one may have in an annuity they own -- if they move those funds to his investment firm. Hmmm... maybe this partly explains how he is a multi-Billionaire!

There's nothing wrong with fees in and of themselves. In fact, I and thousands of other investment advisor reps across the country charge fees for assets under management (AUM) as well. It's the fastest-growing way to be compensated in the financial world (as opposed to being paid trading commissions like the old days).

Even the US government prefers fees over commissions, despite fees being way more expensive for clients over time. The added value must exceed the fee though.

In my personal practice, my clients pay fees to our firm for assets that we manage for them in the stock and bond markets based on their risk tolerance. How much risk do they want to take for potentially higher returns?

Our firm is one of the larger Registered Investment Advisory (RIA) firms in the country and we do an excellent job managing client portfolios. As an aside, one of the points that make us different is that we can use multiple investment strategies within a single account.

Anyway, since he is a fiduciary like I am and must put his client's interests before his own, I have a lot of important questions for him, and you should have them too:

1) Where are you going to put your client's money that is protected from stock market risk and can earn respectable returns?

2) What investments are you going to tell your non-multimillionaire clients (minimum investment with him is $500,000 according to his TV, radio, and print ads) to place money that they cannot afford to lose?

3) What investments do you offer to take the sequence of returns risk from the table?

4) Which of your investments totally eliminate bond interest rate risk and bond default risk?

Other than money market accounts, he doesn't have one!

In my mind, an advisor cannot truly be a fiduciary and have 100% of the clients' best interest at heart, if one advises every single person (through advertising) that all annuities have no place in any income portfolio.

In fact, the best academic research (more studies are added annually) clearly shows that "blanket" statement is false. In my opinion, he's a glorified "pitchman" for his money management firm.

Let me briefly describe how most FIXED INDEXED ANNUITIES (FIA's) work and avoid stock market risk.

Once we've learned how these general types (FIAs) work, then we can see how I use the sub-category of FIAs that I call "Buffer annuities" fit in retirement income plans and taking Required Minimum Distributions (RMDs) and/or improving on the 4% rule — so it can actually work!

As the name fixed indexed annuity implies, the interest "return" is determined by an index or indexes such as the S&P 500, Dow, or the Barclays Bond index.

Once you pay your annuity premium to the insurance company, the company invests those premium dollars into their general account, which is mostly invested in high-quality bonds that pay interest.

The insurer could pay you an interest rate as a CD from what it earns on its bond investments minus its overhead, expenses, and profit margin. Your bank does something very similar in that it pays the depositor an interest rate that depends on its loan portfolio interest income minus its overhead, expenses, and profit margin.

Many FIAs will offer their policyholders a one-year fixed

rate of 1.6% or so (fixed account) right now. Better than most banks, but not very appealing to most folks or... frankly, to me.

As the owner of an FIA, you have the right to forego getting that fixed interest rate and have those interest payments buy options on an index(es) such as the S&P 500, NASDAQ, etc.

By using options, you can participate in the upside of the index when it goes up. But there is a catch – you don't get all or even most of the "upside" in a good year.

Because of the option strategy(s) you choose, you are "limited" in the amount of interest that can be credited to your annuity by a "cap," "spread," or a certain "participation" rate. I'll get to these terms in a moment.

Also, you can never get a loss by using options instead of investing your actual principal since your funds were never invested in the market. And the worst thing that can happen with the option strategies the insurer uses, is that the options expire worthless. When that happens, no interest is credited to your policy that year. In other words, you get a zero return.

When the indexes crash like in 2000, 2001, 2002, and 2008, ZERO is your hero! It's much better to get NO return... than to experience a big loss. Your principal can never go backward due to losses in an index. There is no sequence of return risk either.

And when the index goes up because of the use of options, your gain is limited by a cap, spread, or a participation rate.

A "cap" is the <u>most</u> the interest will credit one year (say 7%), based on the index used, the cost of the options, and the amount the insurance company can spend on the options (which is about equal to the interest they would have paid you in the fixed account).

A "participation rate" (par rate) means that you would get a certain percentage of the index's gain, such as 55%. A participation rate can give you the potential for more upside in a BIG year.

So, with a participation rate of 55%, if the index went up by 6%, your policy would be credited with an interest rate of 3.3% that year. When the index earns 11.2%, with a 55% par rate, your interest credit would be 6.105%. You never participate in any index losses, so zero is your hero.

Like participation rates, a "spread" also allows for some more potential gains when the index has big gains. With a "spread," the insurer uses that spread percentage to buy more options. A 2.75% spread means that you don't get any interest credited unless the index beats that amount (the spread).

You get ALL of the gains above that amount credited to your policy. For example, if the index does 7.75%, with a 2.75% spread, your account would be credited with 5%

interest. If the index returned 11%, you would get credited 8.25%. If the index only did 2%, the spread is larger than the gain and you would get no interest that year. You never have to endure a market-based loss.

Now, the SECRET SAUCE my three bond hedge fund alternatives (Buffer annuities) use is that they give YOU the option every year to pay a little bit (an optional fee) so the insurance company can buy more options. What does that do for you? It gives you more UPSIDE.

It gives you higher PARTICIPATION rates, lower SPREADS, or higher CAPS!

There are two additional attractive features of all FIAs which you should know about. These features set them apart from almost every other type of investment.

They are called the lock-in feature and the annual reset.

The "annual lock-in" feature says that once interest is credited to your account, it becomes principal, and at that point is never subject to future market losses.

Those gains become part of your protected account value. In most cases, on every policy anniversary, any interest gained is credited to your account automatically and becomes principal.

The only way to lock in gains of hedge funds, stocks, bonds, mutual funds, real estate, etc., is to sell the asset.

Of course, unless the asset is inside an IRA or similar IRS-qualified account, there will be a tax due on the gain.

In every annuity, there is no tax due until money is withdrawn. This is an important advantage if you are using investments from your taxable bucket to fund your FIA before retiring and not taking income yet

You won't get a 1099 tax form nor owe any tax until taking income out.

Here is an illustration of the Lock-in and Reset. The S&P 500 is the line that has big ups and downs. An FIA with a 4% cap is the smoother ride.

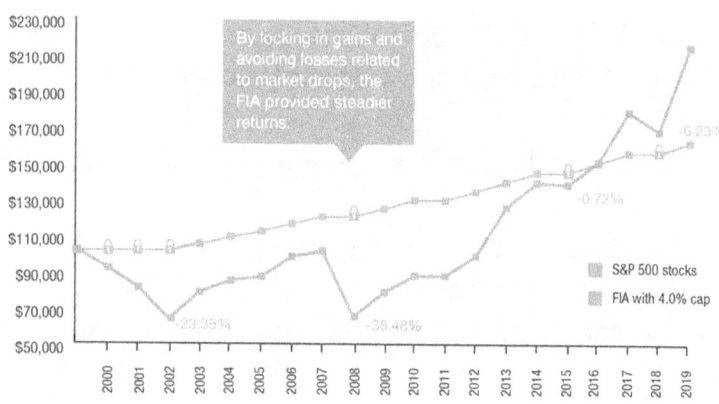

The other nice feature is the "annual reset." This means that the beginning value(s) of the index or indexes you choose to allocate your funds into each policy year resets to the level where the indexes ended the previous year.

This is a very valuable feature.

How is this important? Let's go back to October 16, 2007, and say you rolled over your 401(k) to buy a $400,000 FIA and had 100% of your index allocated to the S&P 500 index when the S&P 500 index closed at 1538 that day. A year later, on October 16, 2008 (your 1st policy anniversary), the S&P index closed at 946... a -38% loss.

As you know, because your principal was never invested in the market, your $400,000 did not lose a dime. Zero was your hero. But this is where annual reset comes into play.

For your next policy year, the index "resets" to where it ended the year before – at 946. Now, all of next year's interest which will be credited to your policy is calculated from that index value to where the index closes a year later – not on the original index price of 1538 when you bought the annuity.

On October 16, 2009, the S&P 500 index closed at 1087. That is a 14.9% gain (subject to participation rates, caps, and/or spreads) and would be the basis of your interest credited to your policy that year. And now, for the next policy year, 1087 would reset to be the starting index value. This is very powerful – especially when accumulating retirement assets.

It doesn't work that way with hedge funds, stocks, or mutual funds. If you retired and rolled over your 401(k) and bought $400,000 of the Vanguard S&P 500 mutual fund on October 16, 2007, (there is no annual lock-in nor is there an annual reset). Your mutual fund would have lost all -38% that the index did in the first year you owned it. Your mutual fund lost a whopping $152,000.

And you would need a +61% gain in the index to just get you back to breakeven (from a -38% loss). Your principal is never protected with most investments, and your past gains are never locked in either. FIAs protect your principal during a market crash and can perform pretty well during recovery periods.

In fact, five years after you bought that mutual fund, the S&P 500 index had still _not_ reached the level where you initially invested (1538). On October 16, 2012, the index closed at 1455 (still well below 2007).

The annual lock-in and reset features can undoubtedly offset some of the disadvantages of not getting the full market gains in big up years due to the caps, spreads, and participation rates inherent in all fixed indexed annuities.

All FIAs offer the potential for respectable gains when the index(es) do well but protects you from all losses and the sequence of returns risk when the markets go down.

In addition to many indexes available with caps, spreads, and participation rates, there are "time periods" that are used to measure potential returns and interest credited.

As just discussed, annual point to point calculates the index return from the day your policy gets issued (your effective date) to a year later (your policy anniversary), and does so year after year. The index value at the start of the policy year is compared to one year later (subject to the caps, etc.).

Some policies only count index gains (lock-in and reset, too) every two or even three years in order to determine your interest earned. There is also monthly averaging, monthly sum, and daily averaging indexing calculations. I'm sure there are other methods too.

Now that you have a better understanding of how fixed indexed annuities work in general, let's take a closer look at some of the past returns in Buffer annuities.

Again, Buffer annuities are designed for accumulation, and for savvy RMD/withdrawal planning -- but not for a guaranteed lifetime income like many FIAs bought today.

Why don't we begin by taking a closer look at my bond hedge fund alternative with my client Joe?

Let's say Joe never wants to pay any fees and is just looking to have slow and steady growth – without any market risk and does not want to pay any fees for more significant potential returns. That's OK, no problem

He decides to invest $100,000. Here is the range of past returns based on my suggested index allocation (for diversification) with NO FEES – zero costs.

In this allocation (Chart 1 below), I diversified with the five indexes — 50% in the one-year allocation and the rest in the 2-year indexes. That is why the biggest returns tend to be in the "even" years rather than the "odd" years.

The 2-year always has higher potential returns due to higher participation rates, – BUT we have to wait two years to see what we earned and get the interest credited to our account.

BUT I like to get at least some return every year, which is why I usually put at least 25%-50% of the funds in the 1-yr allocation. But you can put some, all, or nothing in the one-year allocation.

You get to decide precisely how you want to reallocate within the funds each year. I want your account to grow safely! (I'm always happy to make recommendations).

Learn what's in it for me at the end of this book. You can decide what, if any, fees (to buy more upside with more money to buy options), you're willing to pay each year for a potential higher return.

The left box is the most recent ten calendar years, the middlebox is the best 10-year period out of the last 20 years (some 2,000 tested periods), and the box on the right is the worst 10-year period out of the last 20 years.

Again, there are no fees in the 1st first chart below. The next ten years will not look the same as the last ten years. I think they won't be as good... but they could be better.

When including this CONSERVATIVE allocation inside one of my retirement income plans, I'm using very conservative average annual gains of only 5% – which is about 70% of the worst 10-year period was and well below the other two boxes. That 5% future returns figure is higher than what most believe the Bond Index will provide - with less risk.

If actual returns are better than that – the RMD plan becomes better as well. Remember that since 50% of the funds are in the 2-yr bucket; they never get any interest credited until the end of the 2nd year.

Now, these indexes did NOT exist 20 years ago but back-tested using the same rules-based algorithms for determining the investments within each index.

Of course, future returns are not guaranteed (other than a 0% return when markets go down) and will likely be very different than shown.

Bonds, bond mutual funds, and bond ETTs have NO guarantees at all, have more risk, and have higher expenses. Nor do hedge funds! And you will notice there are pretty similar returns across the board (both good and bad) over the 10-year period in the most recent, highest, and lowest charts right below.

In chart #1, the lowest (worst past ten years would have been 7.15% average returns, and the most recent ten years would have been 8.41%.

Chart #1

NON-GUARANTEED ANNUITY CONTRACT VALUES
INDEX GROWTH PERIOD COMPARISON - MOST RECENT, HIGH, LOW

The Annual Effective Rates reflect initial allocations and application of current Index Strategy Rates to historical index returns, unless otherwise noted. The Accumulation Value reflects selected withdrawal activity.

Annual Effective Rate Most Recent: 8.41%+

Annual Effective Rate Highest: 10.82%+

Annual Effective Rate Lowest: 7.15%+

Contract Year	MOST RECENT		HIGHEST		LOWEST	
	Credited Interest Rate	Accumulation Value	Credited Interest Rate	Accumulation Value	Credited Interest Rate	Accumulation Value
At Issue		$100,000		$100,000		$100,000
1	3.76%	$103,763	5.41%	$105,409	2.39%	$102,390
2	13.66%	$117,937	25.00%	$131,762	2.52%	$104,972
3	4.63%	$123,400	3.57%	$136,467	2.76%	$107,867
4	5.55%	$130,243	14.74%	$156,580	9.74%	$118,372
5	2.84%	$133,946	3.67%	$162,328	2.27%	$121,062
6	23.24%	$165,074	11.99%	$181,796	14.90%	$139,100
7	0.05%	$165,158	1.87%	$184,825	4.46%	$145,310
8	17.92%	$194,752	21.24%	$224,074	22.29%	$177,705
9	2.72%	$200,041	1.63%	$227,724	2.02%	$181,286
10	12.13%	$224,302	22.65%	$279,298	10.05%	$199,507
Annual Effective Rate	**8.41%+**		**10.82%+**		**7.15%+**	

I would expect average annual returns of between 5.5%-7% over the next ten years.

Maybe not such exciting returns compared to stocks, are they? But they crush CD returns at any bank and will likely outperform bond funds – with less credit risk, interest rate risk, and inflation risk. No fees, no expenses. No credit or interest rate risk either.

Let's look at the same annuity, but with "some" optional fees to buy more upside and potentially better gains. Again – there are mandatory NO fees or expenses at all.

So, Mary is OK with paying "some" fees since she pays her advisor to manage her money now.

In Chart #2, the returns are based on my suggested index allocation (diversification). Half of the indexes have NO FEES and the other half (optional fee) costing 1% annually – for an overall net fee cost of 0.5%.

The optional fees allow for higher potential returns (better participation rates/caps/spreads) – while your worst return is 0% in any year – except for any optional fee charged for purchasing more upside potential (more options).

Again, I split 50/50 between the one and 2-year allocations. Recall there are higher potential returns in the 2-year allocation — which is why you will notice the bigger returns in the "even" years as the 2-year allocations only get the interest credited at the end of the 2nd year.

Earnings would be smoother but likely lower if 100% of the funds were in the 1-yr buckets.

There is no interest credited to any allocation in the 2-yr indexes until the end of the 2nd year. BUT I like to get at least some return every year, so I usually put at least 25%-50% of the principal in the 1-yr allocation.

You get to decide however you want to allocate the funds every single year.

Again, the left box is the most recent ten calendar years, the middlebox is the best 10-year period out of the last 20 years (some 2,000 tested periods), and the right box is the worst 10-year period out of the previous 20 years.

The returns shown below are NET of the 0.5% annual fees (optional) returns the investor gets to keep. The next ten years will not look the same as the last ten years. I think they won't be as good… but they could be better.

In chart #2, the lowest (worst past ten years) would have been 8.16% average returns, and the most recent calendar ten years would have been 9.64%.

Since I don't think the next ten years will be as good as the last ten, I would expect average annual NET returns of between 6.5%-8% over the next ten years. – even after the 0.5% optional annual fee (only 50% of the acct @1% fee).

Chart #2

NON-GUARANTEED ANNUITY CONTRACT VALUES
INDEX GROWTH PERIOD COMPARISON - MOST RECENT, HIGH, LOW

The Annual Effective Rates reflect initial allocations and application of current Index Strategy Rates to historical index returns, unless otherwise noted. The Accumulation Value reflects strategy fees and selected withdrawal activity.

Contract Year	MOST RECENT		HIGHEST		LOWEST	
	Credited Interest Rate*	Accumulation Value	Credited Interest Rate*	Accumulation Value	Credited Interest Rate*	Accumulation Value
At Issue		$100,000		$100,000		$100,000
1	4.82%	$104,568	6.91%	$106,662	2.39%	$102,141
2	15.63%	$120,130	31.09%	$139,033	4.37%	$105,843
3	5.47%	$126,395	4.30%	$144,677	3.00%	$108,756
4	6.87%	$134,146	17.07%	$168,221	11.37%	$120,301
5	3.41%	$138,398	4.36%	$175,139	4.40%	$125,292
6	28.17%	$176,325	15.84%	$201,432	16.75%	$145,329
7	0.02%	$175,909	1.99%	$204,953	3.86%	$150,556
8	22.58%	$214,239	24.45%	$253,312	27.51%	$190,816
9	4.65%	$223,667	3.06%	$260,446	2.52%	$195,150
10	13.03%	$250,985	28.90%	$333,456	13.30%	$219,502
Annual Effective Rate	10.13%+		13.31%+		8.68%+	
Net Annual Effective Rate	9.64%^		12.80%^		8.18%^	

Annual Effective Rate Most Recent: 10.13%+

Annual Effective Rate Highest: 13.31%+

Annual Effective Rate Lowest: 8.68%+

Keep in mind that since 50% of the funds are in the 2-yr bucket, they never get any interest credited until the end of the 2nd year. And again, no sequence of return risk.

These past returns are a lot more exciting when compared to bond funds. In fact, even the worst 10-yr period above (right column) beat the total returns of the S&P 500 index from 2000-2011 – which were under 3% annualized for that time period. And it had four big negative years too.

And finally, Michael has NO issue with paying fees (to buy more options) for the potential for much greater returns. Since his downside is protected (0% floor), he's willing to pay the fee on all indexes to get the enhanced potential. Here are returns based on my suggested index allocation (diversification), with ALL the indexes having (optional) fees costing 1% annually.

The optional fees allow for higher potential returns – while your worst return is 0% in any year. That excludes any optional fee (1%) to purchase more upside potential.

The 3rd chart has all the funds invested in the 2-year allocations – so no interest is credited to the policy until the end of every 2nd year (see 0% on the odd years).

You always get to decide however you want to allocate your funds each year. I'm always happy and dedicated to helping with recommendations. The following ten years will not look the same as the last ten years. I don't think they will be as good… but they could be even better.

Chart 3

NON-GUARANTEED ANNUITY CONTRACT VALUES
INDEX GROWTH PERIOD COMPARISON - MOST RECENT, HIGH, LOW

The Annual Effective Rates reflect initial allocations and application of current Index Strategy Rates to historical index returns, unless otherwise noted. The Accumulation Value reflects strategy fees and selected withdrawal activity.

Annual Effective Rate Most Recent: 11.97%+

Annual Effective Rate Highest: 17.33%+

Annual Effective Rate Lowest: 11.43%+

Contract Year	MOST RECENT		HIGHEST		LOWEST	
	Credited Interest Rate*	Accumulation Value	Credited Interest Rate*	Accumulation Value	Credited Interest Rate*	Accumulation Value
At Issue		$100,000		$100,000		$100,000
1	0.00%	$100,000	0.00%	$100,000	0.00%	$100,000
2	20.19%	$118,185	58.16%	$156,160	11.13%	$109,130
3	0.00%	$118,185	0.00%	$156,160	0.00%	$109,130
4	16.58%	$135,414	26.98%	$195,144	15.15%	$123,476
5	0.00%	$135,414	0.00%	$195,144	0.00%	$123,476
6	40.41%	$187,424	28.10%	$246,072	24.06%	$150,714
7	0.00%	$187,424	0.00%	$246,072	0.00%	$150,714
8	29.89%	$237,815	31.34%	$318,276	44.79%	$215,203
9	0.00%	$237,815	0.00%	$318,276	0.00%	$215,203
10	22.21%	$285,869	46.31%	$459,312	28.39%	$271,993
Annual Effective Rate	11.97%+		17.33%+		11.43%+	
Net Annual Effective Rate	11.08%^		16.47%^		10.52%^	

Like before, the left box is the most recent ten calendar years, the middlebox is the best 10-year period out of the last 20 years (some 2,000 tested daily periods), and the box on the right is the worst 10-year period out of the last 20 years.

The returns shown below are NET of the 1% annual fees (optional) – returns the investor gets to keep. This time there is 100% in the 2-yr allocation, which is why the only returns are in the "even" years.

This is a more AGGRESSIVE allocation (more like a real hedge fund). Those are much higher returns than what most believe the Bond Index or most bond funds will provide and are closer to equity-type returns with much less risk.

Using all fees, I'd project something like an 8%-10% avg annual return over ten years. That's 3X the total return of the S&P 500 from 2000-2011 (including dividends). However, even a 5% average return will likely crush bonds.

Do you see the 44% gain in the LOWEST column (right) in year 4? And then the other 2-year gains of 24% and 28% gains in years 6 and 10?

In real life, for more "aggressive" investors, I'd probably design this to have 50% in the 1-year bucket the first year only and then switch to 100% in the 2-yr buckets. So, I'd have a 2-yr bucket (50%) coming due with interest earned every single year. You'd get lower total participation rates but should earn interest almost every year.

Again, these returns assume we never make educated changes in the indexes based on the economy and markets. With some changes made over time, I'd suspect the returns could be even greater.

Remember to think of this as a "Principal Protected" account – where your worst return is 0%! You can never experience a loss induced by the market. Yet you have plenty of upside. Just look at the growth in all scenarios.

The only "loss" you can ever have is up to a 1% reduction in account value if you decide to put 100% of the funds in the index managed by Fidelity (1 or 2 years) and the index's return was less than 0%.

I forgot to mention one HUGE fact regarding the optional fee of 1% should you ever decide to take advantage of gaining more upside. Oh, this is cool.

If you use it and at the end of your ten years, you paid more in fees than you got in gains, they would bring you back to even (as if you never paid the fees at all).

Let me explain it this way. Say you invest $100,000. If you paid 1% in fees for 100% of your index allocation every year (AGGRESSIVE allocation)... and each and every one of the indexes went down every single year at the end of the ten years, you could actually walk away with your entire $100,000 back.

In other words, they would refund all fees paid to get you back to where you started.

Not likely to ever be needed or used – but it is guaranteed. I think that is very fair, don't you?

One client told me that's like gambling with no risk of loss. Try to get that guarantee in Las Vegas!

Of course, this is not for everyone or every situation for sure. No financial strategy or product is or ever will be.

But I believe that it is certainly worth exploring for at least a portion of your bond portfolio, given the current state of interest rates and their foreseeable future. It is an attractive CD alternative too.

We (my wife Norma) moved about 50% of her account that our firm manages at TD Ameritrade into two of these bond alternatives. The remaining 50% are still at TD now in stock ETFs and funds, and we can be more aggressive.

I certainly would never recommend it to you if it does not perfectly align with your own goals and personal circumstances. I'm a fiduciary and always must, and do... put my clients' best interests first.

I mentioned using 2-3 hedge fund alternatives, so I'll just add a quick summary of another one. It's my slightly more diversified allocation than the other "Poor man's hedge fund" that I just described, and I use it when clients don't want 100% of their bond alternative to be in one annuity.

This example uses a $100,000 initial investment and is shown on Chart #4.

Chart #4

Most Recent 10

The **Most Recent 10** index scenario reflects the performance of the annuity assuming the historical performance of the index over the most recent 10 calendar year period.

Contract Year	Assumed Interest Rate	Accumulated Value
1	N/A	$98,250
2	58.59%	$153,092
3	N/A	$150,413
4	14.96%	$169,972
5	N/A	$166,997
6	46.98%	$240,363
7	N/A	$236,156
8	24.34%	$286,774
9	N/A	$281,755
10	30.49%	$363,640

Product Geometric Mean Interest Rate* = 15.80%
Annual Growth Rate Net of Charges** = 13.78%

Highest

The **Highest** index scenario reflects the performance of the annuity during a continuous period of 10 years out of the last 20 years where the index had the highest 10 year growth.

Contract Year	Assumed Interest Rate	Accumulated Value
1	N/A	$98,250
2	42.72%	$137,765
3	N/A	$135,355
4	15.46%	$153,515
5	N/A	$150,829
6	46.58%	$217,850
7	N/A	$214,038
8	35.02%	$278,869
9	N/A	$273,989
10	62.15%	$435,831

Product Geometric Mean Interest Rate* = 17.92%
Annual Growth Rate Net of Charges** = 15.86%

Lowest

The **Lowest** index scenario reflects the performance of the annuity during a continuous period of 10 years out of the last 20 years where the index had the lowest 10 year growth.

Contract Year	Assumed Interest Rate	Accumulated Value
1	N/A	$98,250
2	8.31%	$104,548
3	N/A	$102,719
4	17.61%	$119,142
5	N/A	$117,058
6	19.39%	$138,220
7	N/A	$135,801
8	53.45%	$205,945
9	N/A	$202,341
10	9.77%	$220,971

Product Geometric Mean Interest Rate* = 10.17%
Annual Growth Rate Net of Charges** = 8.25%

In this annuity, rather than ten years, it's only a 7-year commitment, and like the other, you can take 10% out every year without any penalty whatsoever.

In this past 10-yrs performance, I have used all 2-year buckets (for more upside) and all three indexes with the annual fee (1.75%) to buy more upside. Again, I don't think the next ten years will be as good as the last 10 in the stock market. So, I wouldn't expect the returns here to be as good either.

Even the LOWEST 10-year period this Buffer annuity had a 53% gain plus a 17% and 19% year and overall average of over 8.25% annually NET of fees.

You'll notice in all three boxes, in the first year, the value is less than the $100,000 invested. That's due to the fee taken out every year, but no interest is credited in 2-year allocations until the end of the second year.

And in all examples above, I made no changes to the initial index allocations. That is not realistic. Normally I would, based on what's going on in the economy. Do you keep your 401K invested the same way every year?

But the most recent returns shown in the above charts will have crushed a number of expensive hedge funds and the typical 60%/40% retiree equity portfolios as well – and did so without any market risk. Buffer annuities can compete with stock funds, but for most folks, I position them as a bond alternative.

One of the three indexes that I use in this Buffer annuity is "run" by IBM's Watson supercomputer. It picks the best 250 stocks out of the USA's biggest 1000 companies.

Another index is an offshoot of the NASDAQ, while the 3rd is a multi-asset class index. If I wanted the returns in the above chart to look better, I'd put 100% in the NASDAQ-type index (instead of 40%) and 0% in the multi-asset (rather than 30%). But again, I like to diversify.

The main point of this chapter and charts was to show how your principal is protected and that you have the advantage of the reset mechanism to help you when the markets crash (in that your indexes don't have to get back to the pre-crash levels to start making returns again).

Unlike the stock market, market volatility is truly your friend with Buffer annuities.

Why is that?

Again, because of the lock-in and reset. When the markets crash, your FIA is protected by the 0% floor. Not only that, the indexes reset on your policy anniversary, and your future gains are determined by the lower levels on the lock-in and reset.

As I wrote earlier, financial products are like golf clubs. They simply help you get around the golf course with as good a score as you are capable of. They are a means to an end. A tool to help you achieve your financial goals.

You don't want only to have a putter or a driver and use that ONE club for every shot you make over the 18 holes. That's why you carry a full bag of clubs. Financial products are no different.

Annuities, mutual funds, ETFs, stocks, bonds, insurance should be more than just products. They should be SOLUTIONS to financial problems or worries. If they don't solve a problem, then you don't need them. Period.

If you are not a golfer, think about household tools. If you need to make a hole in the wall, you use a drill – not a hammer. If you need to saw a piece of wood in half, a hammer won't do a good job – but a saw will!

As a financial advisor for the past 20+ years, I've been using the "right" golf club or financial tool to solve client problems and fears or to take advantage of opportunities. So I use hammers when that tool solves a particular problem and a saw for another financial problem.

Clients want personalized solutions – not products.
Part of my job is uncovering clients' fears, doubts, and uncertainties. The things that keep them up at night.

Buffer annuities can solve the problem inherent in bonds. Rising interest rates can cause the value of bonds to fall. Bonds also have credit risk and definite maturities which, produces reinvestment-rate risk. Bonds also have fixed coupon rates. Buffer annuities don't have those issues. But no financial product is perfect. Nothing ever is.

And even if someone was not too worried about the bonds in their portfolio, I'd venture to guess that the returns (without market risk) will be higher in them over time verses bonds.

As we'll see in a moment, Buffer annuities can solve problems with Required Minimum Distributions (RMDs) when stock portfolios are falling and hold their value when interest rates rise and as bonds lose value.

January 20, 2021. Here's Morningstar's take on the likely future of bonds going forward: "Bond-market bulls are few and far between, too. While a 60/40 portfolio composed of U.S. large caps and investment-grade bonds has been tough to beat over the past decade, most of the firms in our survey are forecasting constrained returns for those asset classes going forward."

It's worth noting that in playing hockey, you want to skate to where the puck is going – not where it's been. That's what the pro players do.

It's the same with investing. The 30-year bull market in bonds (rising bond values - with interest rates declining over that time) is probably over. Let's look forward and skate to where interest rates and bond prices are likely going to be down the road.

Comments like the above and those at the start of the book from JPMorgan and Bank of America (essentially saying that the "60/40 portfolio is dead" can be a problem for folks in or near retirement. So we need to find appropriate solutions to make their retirement income both larger and safer.

But as I wrote earlier, it's not just the bond component of the 60/40 portfolio that is becoming worrisome. So are equities.

I've previously written about the CAPE ratio and how it predicts future returns in the stock market. Although Buffer annuities are not meant to compete against stock returns, it wouldn't surprise me if they did win that race over the next decade. Why?

Even though the Buffer annuity indexes are based on various equity-based indexes, the stock market does not offer protection from market losses, lock-in, and reset.

You can see on the previous chart how high the Shiller CAPE ratio is on a historical basis. It's not quite as high as before the huge dot.com bust of 2000, but it's getting closer. That chart was produced on June 23, 2021, but the CAPE ratio is about the same in February 2022.

So not only are bond values in danger of falling should interest rates rise, but many would say that the stock market might be overvalued as well with the CAPE ratio at its highest level in about 20 years.

As indicated earlier in this book, the higher the CAPE ratio, the more likely future returns will be lower. And Vanguard's projections on the upcoming chart seem to bear that out.

Does your stock advisor or portfolio manager have a plan for reworking the 60/40 portfolio in times like this? Although it's beyond the scope of this book, our firm does.

I might add this point, that Index Universal Life (IULs) insurance policies (or even whole life insurance) could also, be great alternatives to bonds. IULs work in the same manner that FIAs do with a 0% floor – but have higher caps and participation rates.

I call IULs my TRIPLE ZERO™ plans as they are ROTH alternatives – 1) ZERO income/contribution limits 2) ZERO market risk and 3) ZERO income taxes when you play by the IRS rules.

You can buy my book "[TAX-FREE Millionaire](#)" on KINDLE or paperback at amazon which only explains TRIPLE ZERO™ plans... or the expanded version ["Get Me to ZERO"](#) which describes <u>seven</u> strategies for a tax-free retirement (including the full description of TRIPLE ZERO™ plans).

Life insurance cannot be held inside of an IRA, so we have to use non-IRA money to fund one. And to be tax-free, we have to follow the IRS rules about funding the policy over a minimum of 4 years (rather than a lump sum premium made into a Buffer annuity).

Like Buffer annuities, only a few IUL policies allow you to pay a fee to buy more options and get more upside – but they are available. But life insurance does not have RMDs, so although you can take tax-free distributions from your specially-designed policy to help fund your retirement lifestyle, it doesn't solve the RMD and 4% rule issues.

Our firm has other <u>non-insurance-based</u> bond-alternative strategies too, which are beyond the scope of this book.

Vanguard's Market Projections

Take a look at what Mutual Fund giant Vanguard thinks is ahead for the markets over the next ten years on the next chart! It's nothing like the last ten years for sure.

What do you think about Vanguard's latest projections for the next decade's various stock and bond markets? It's pretty depressing, isn't it?

Asset-class return outlooks

Our 10-year, annualized, nominal return projections are shown below. The categories marked with an asterisk (*) reflect a February 28, 2022, running of the Vanguard Capital Markets Model® (VCMM) for broad equity and fixed income asset classes only. Outlooks for the remaining sub-asset classes reflect a December 31, 2021, running of the VCMM. Please note that the figures are based on a 1.0-point range around the rounded 50th percentile of the distribution of return outcomes for equities and a 0.5-point range around the rounded 50th percentile for fixed income.

Equities	Return projection	Median volatility
U.S. equities*	2.8%–4.8%	16.8%
Global equities ex-U.S. (unhedged)*	5.7%–7.7%	18.4%
U.S. value	2.8%–4.8%	19.0%
U.S. growth	−1.2%–−0.8%	17.5%
U.S. large-cap	1.9%–3.9%	16.3%
U.S. small-cap	2.3%–4.3%	22.2%
U.S. real estate investment trusts	1.8%–3.8%	19.2%
Global ex-U.S. developed markets equities (unhedged)	5.1%–7.1%	16.3%
Emerging markets equities (unhedged)	4.3%–6.3%	26.8%

Fixed income	Return projection	Median volatility
U.S. aggregate bonds*	1.9%–2.9%	4.6%
U.S. Treasury bonds*	1.6%–2.6%	4.8%
U.S. credit bonds*	2.4%–3.4%	5.8%
U.S. cash*	1.5%–2.5%	1.1%
Global bonds ex-U.S. (hedged)*	1.8%–2.8%	3.9%
U.S. high-yield corporate bonds	2.3%–3.3%	10.3%
U.S. Treasury Inflation-Protected Securities	1.2%–2.2%	4.6%
Emerging markets sovereign	2.5%–3.5%	10.5%
U.S. inflation	1.6%–2.6%	2.3%

These probabilistic return assumptions depend on current market conditions and, as such, may change over time.

IMPORTANT: The projections or other information generated by the Vanguard Capital Markets Model® regarding the likelihood of various investment outcomes are hypothetical in nature, do not reflect actual investment results, and are not guarantees of future results. Distribution of return outcomes from the VCMM are derived from 10,000 simulations for each modeled asset class. Simulations are as of February 28, 2022, and December 31, 2021. Results from the model may vary with each use and over time. For more information, see the Notes section.

Source: Vanguard Investment Strategy Group.

Vanguard seems to be making it pretty clear to diversify your portfolio with investments that cannot go down – without even saying so. Ones with a 0% floor so you can avoid market losses. And ones that lock in gains and can reset to take advantage of the market volatility. By the way, the "Medium Volatility" column means that in any given year, the expected range of returns might be 16.8% (for US Equities) above or below the expected range of returns shown for each type of asset.

So in any given year, US Equities might return between -14% to +21.6% (with only medium volatility, which means about two-thirds of the years). Of course, returns could be way worse than we saw in 2008 (-37%) or way better, as in 2019 (+30%).

Vanguard is projecting that with all those likely gains and losses, you should plan on your US equities to only average that 2.8%-4.8% over that time period – including having years with big losses and big gains over the next decade.

Suppose the stock market only averages 3%-5% annually for the next ten years, as Vanguard (and others) predict. In that case, you might also need some different non-annuity strategies for that side of your portfolio.

Did you notice what Vanguard projects for bond returns over the next decade? All types of bond offerings range from 2% for TIPS to 3.3% for risky high-yield "junk" bonds. Buffer annuities should absolutely trounce those meager projected returns of bonds.

Yet, despite meager current bond interest rates (and low for the last 5+ years) and projected returns going forward, look at how investor money is flowing into bond funds and ETFs. Truly buying high (and likely selling lower).

Bond & Equity Cumulative Flows

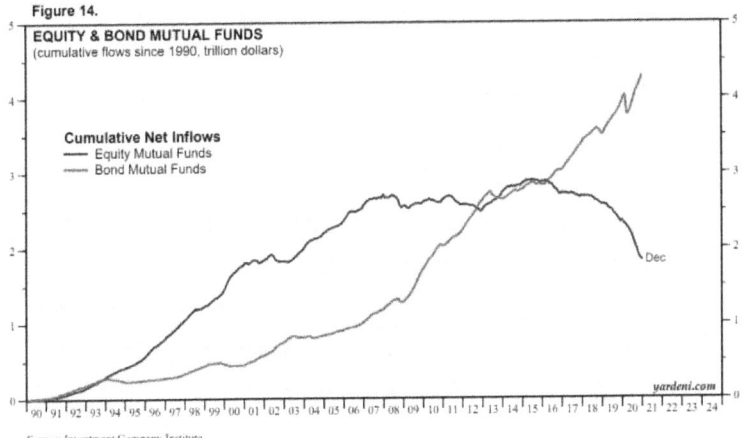

Bond inflows is the line sloping <u>upward</u> on the far right.

Why on earth are investors flocking to bond funds at times like this? It makes no sense to me at all! If rates rise, the bond values will fall. If they don't rise, our current rates don't even keep up with inflation (now 7%).

Again, our advisory firm has some proven ideas for other bond alternatives and less volatile stock strategies that you might want to hear more about. Why?

A few pages back, I mentioned how people have fears, doubts, and uncertainties with their retirement planning. That's entirely natural, as paychecks from working cease. It seems to me that they are looking for hope, peace of mind, stability, freedom, independence, simplicity, and any other intangible needs.

Well, here are some reasons that my clients told me why they wanted my help:

- "We're afraid I'm not doing the right things with my money. There's too much conflicting information out there."
- "I just want to simplify my investments since it's too frustrating to keep up with them all."
- "I don't think you can ever have enough money."
- "We want to keep the same lifestyle in retirement as we had when we were working."
- "I definitely don't want to end up like my folks – old, watching every single dollar, and always worried."
- "I don't want to be weighed down with details."
- "I don't want to pay any more taxes than I have to."
- "This is the first time we've ever retired. We don't want to mess it up."
- "I want to make sure my family is taken care of – especially my wife, if I go first."
- "We don't want for us to be a burden on our children."
- "What accounts should we withdraw from first?"
- "I want an advisor to help keep me on course and not let me be distracted by headlines and emotions."

I always ask my clients what they want out of their money and their life (goals) and then help them stay on track and overcome the bumps we know will happen along the way. Bumps are just part of life.

Anyway, let's get back to the subject at hand and perhaps the most important part of the book – taking income.

OK, next is where we talk about how to use these Buffer annuities when taking income for your retirement lifestyle above and beyond what you would get from Social Security or any pension(s) you may have.

My RMD and Withdrawal Strategy

So far, we've seen the past returns of the bond-alternative Buffer annuities and learned how they work.

You've seen why many financial professionals think that the traditional 60%/40% portfolios are "dead." Most of the concern has been on the bond side of the portfolio.

But Vanguard's stock and bond predictions for the coming decade make both sides of your portfolio look suspect.

You've learned about (or have been reminded about) the "4% Rule" – as a rule of thumb of how much you can take out of your savings each year, adjusted by inflation.

However, no matter what returns you AVERAGE over your retirement, it's the sequence of those returns that will largely determine the success or failure of the 4% rule or whatever withdrawal rate you deem appropriate.

And I haven't even written about tax-smart portfolio strategies in this book! Most folks spend too much time worrying about their returns and not enough on being tax-savvy. We all need to pay our fair share, but why pay more to the IRS than you need to?

Now it's time to see how I use Buffer annuities in client portfolios regarding smart Required Minimum Distribution (RMD) and withdrawal strategies.

It's time to learn how to replace a good portion of your bonds with these Buffer annuities to increase your overall returns while decreasing interest rate and credit risks.

Let's begin with a quick analogy.

You are on the top floor of a 55-story building, and you want to get down to the lobby safely. You have two choices. Yes, there is a third choice (the stairwell), but most of us wouldn't even consider this option unless there's a fire.

The elevator on the right has three cables securing it. The elevator on the left has only one cable. Which elevator are you going to get on? Would you take the first elevator whose doors opened… or would you wait for the elevator on the right with the three cables to take you down?

For most of us (except those thrill-seekers), we'd wait for the more secure elevator. I certainly would.

Well, think of the three cables as a thoughtfully crafted (skating to where the puck is going to be) portfolio of equities, a diverse fixed income strategy (more than just bonds), and Buffer annuities which can take advantage of stock market volatility with the protection of a 0% floor. Maybe 2 strategies for each cable for more diversification.

In our investment advisory firm, we like to use a number of alternative bond strategies that I would call "fixed-income" rather than simply a bond index(s).

We do that to minimize interest rate risk, duration risk, and even credit risk that is inherent in bonds. In fact, we can use several different equity strategies as well to reduce market risk too. They have a great track record.

Our firm manages some $8 BILLION in over 30,000 client accounts in all 50 states. Unlike most firms that focus on the portfolio's stock side, we believe that the fixed income side needs just as much attention.

But as mentioned earlier, portfolio design and investment management are beyond the scope of this book.

Think of the elevator with just one cable as the typical 60/40 portfolio at Vanguard or anywhere else. Please take another look at their projections above again.

Now Vanguard nor any other investment firm cannot truly tell the future, but they certainly have the weight and experience of hundreds of professional market analysts and academic researchers behind them.

Nor can the Nobel-prize winner, Robert Shiller, with his famous CAPE ratio, predict future market returns. But his track record is impressive going back decades. The market will not go up forever without a typical bear market to wash out the speculators.

Anyway, let's review Required Minimum Distributions (RMDs) for traditional IRAs, 401Ks, 403Bs, 457s, SEPs, SIMPLEs, and other deductible retirement plans.

The IRS allowed you to deduct your retirement contributions (within limits) while you were working.

Now, at age 72 (it used to be age 70.5), they want to start collecting the taxes on both your contributions and the investment earnings your accounts have earned for decades.

They make you take out some money every year from age 72 (whether you need the funds or not) - so they can finally TAX you on it.

But the first-year RMD is 3.65%. So, if you have $100,000 total in your IRAs, then you'd have to withdraw $3,650. The following year the percentage of withdrawal goes up and does so every year going forward.

Let me repeat that. Each year, as you get older, the RMD percentage you must take out of your IRA grows a bit. For example, when your age 85, you must take out about 6.76%. At age 92, it's about 10% of your IRA balance(s).

I would expect the new table to be a pretty similar schedule as the old, but I don't have any more insight than anyone else on this. We'll just have to wait and see.

The good thing about RMDs and IRAs is that the IRS

doesn't care which IRA you take the RMD from (if you have more than one). You can take 100% of your total RMD from one IRA and not touch the others or take it out pro-rata from all of them or anything in between.

Keep in mind that RMDs are calculated separately if you are married. So, you'll have your own RMD and your spouse will have their own RMD.

Of course, there are no RMDs if you own any ROTHs.

Please note that the IRS looks at 401Ks, 403Bs, and 457 plans differently for some reason. You must take the RMD from that account only. You cannot take a 401K-based RMD from an IRA account. Crazy. Well, that is the government for you! So, simply roll your 401K into an IRA!

Anyway, that's just another reason why I generally recommend rolling over your savings from a 401K, 403B, etc., to an IRA.

So knowing that you have complete flexibility in where you take your IRA RMDs from; this is how we use Buffer annuities as part of an intelligent withdrawal strategy.

By the way, the withdrawal strategy works even if you are not age 72 yet and are just withdrawing funds from your savings (IRAs or brokerage accounts) to fund your retirement lifestyle. The principle is exactly the same.

The strategy revolves around "buy low" and "sell high."

Or at least don't sell (and withdraw) your RMD or lifestyle money after the market has crashed. Why?

Because once you've withdrawn (sold your stocks) to take your RMD or make a withdrawal for any reason, those shares of stocks can never recover along with the market – since they are no longer in the account (you spent them).

You'll recall that the Buffer annuities can never go down because of the markets. ZERO is your hero in a market crash.

So, here is my foolproof yet straightforward strategy to make sure you never have to sell stocks, mutual funds, and ETFs in a down market to fund your RMD or lifestyle withdrawal. It just takes a little discipline to make the strategy work.

When the previous year's stock market ends higher, you take your **total** RMD (including any RMD necessary from your Buffer annuity) from the stock market account.

Again, we want to sell stocks, funds, etc., when they are higher – not when they lost money (i.e. more than 5%). Take the profits when the market them gives to you. Don't watch them evaporate in the next market crash.

The market goes up 3 out of every 4 years on average, so you'll be taking total RMDs from this account most years. On those 1 out of every four years, on average, when the market drops (ends lower), we take the **total** RMD from the Buffer annuity (since it doesn't get any of the market losses) and let our stock accounts recover. We don't sell when the stocks are low. We let them rise in value again.

If the market stays down for a second year, you take the total RMD out of the Buffer annuity again. And let your stocks recover.

It hardly ever happens that the market is down three years in a row (2000, 2001, and 2002), but if it's necessary, then take the third **total** RMD from the Buffer annuity too.

If you have a number of good years in the market, keep taking your withdrawals from the stock accounts and let the Buffer annuity grow for the next time you'll tap it for income or RMDs.

What Norma and I have done is we took out 40% of her IRA money (rolled over from her 401K) out of our firm's managed account at TD Ameritrade (TDA) and put it into the two Buffer annuities that I described earlier in the book.

We used two Buffer annuities for index diversification, and it made sense with the amount of dollars she invested.

With the money remaining at TDA, we are 80% in equity ETFs and some mutual funds and the other 20% in our firm's alternative fixed income strategies – for better returns than bond index funds (with less risk).

So essentially, we have 48% in stocks – ETFs and mutual funds - (with some hedging for protection) and 40% in Buffer annuities, and 12% in our fixed-income alternatives. And we sleep very well at night.

I expect the returns in the Buffer annuities will do almost as well as the stock market over time since they have the 0% floor protection when the market goes down and the very valuable "lock-in and reset" features.

I'm projecting 6%-7% average NET returns in our Buffer annuities (using my preferred index allocations) which are larger than Vanguard's stock projections for the US markets (let alone their forecast for the bond markets).

I believe they will undoubtedly crush the projected returns of the bond indexes that Vanguard made. For that matter, so will our firm's alternate fixed income strategies.

That's not to say that what we are doing for ourselves would be the right thing for you or anyone else. For example, you might want to take more or less risk.

It's seldom that I recommend something to a client that we don't own ourselves. Of course, there are some ideas or strategies that are not in line with our own goals and circumstances. So, I don't implement those in our own plan since they don't fit the bill for our financial planning.

And you know what else we did? We took the sequence of returns risk off of the table — no "Jill" scenarios.

That about wraps it up for Buffer annuities.

As you have seen, Buffer annuities can have excellent returns (especially if you opt to pay the small fee to buy more upside) – without taking any market risk.

Although they are not hedge funds, they are certainly an appropriate alternative investment instead of bonds, bond mutual funds, and bond ETFs – which all carry interest rate risk and credit risk – while currently suffering from meager returns along the way.

Investors and retirees will have a hard time getting by on 1% to 3% interest rates. Even if rates go up (as they should), then the value of the bonds will fall. Just like a see-saw, when one goes up, the other goes down. And when one side goes down, the other goes up.

Getting average annual returns of 5%, 6%, or higher over time versus bonds (especially if fixed income is 40% to 60% of one's portfolio) can literally rescue a retiree's future.

Those returns might even beat a conservative investor's stock portfolio's returns – and do so without the sequence of returns risk. Of course, that potential outperformance would come from Buffer annuities having the 0% floor and the lock-in and reset features.

You saw from the chart of Vanguard's market predictions for the coming decade of equity returns in the 3% to 5% range and the current high CAPE ratio suggesting flat or even negative returns for the S&P 500 over the next ten years. Maybe it's time to consider taking some of your profits in the stock market off of the table too.

Buffer annuities have no embedded fees or expenses. They are less expensive than the cheapest mutual funds or ETFs while offering more diversification than single stocks. Who doesn't like 0% expenses?

You only pay an optional fee if you want higher potential returns – and you get to make that decision every policy anniversary. You've seen the advantages and results of paying these optional fees in Charts #2 and #3.

And you learned about the 4% rule (if you hadn't known about it already) and why so many market professionals think that it won't work in the future for 60/40 portfolios.

Of course, you'll have to come to your conclusions about those projections based on your thinking.

And then, there is the tax deferral inherent in every type of annuity. I've hardly mentioned tax deferral because about 75% of my clients put IRA-type money into their Buffer annuities.

But using non-qualified (the IRS term for non-IRA-type money) makes sense as well. Tax deferral is a good thing, as you can see from my chart below.

The chart shows the power of putting off paying the taxes.

Although money does not double every year (at least not for 20 years in a row), the chart below illustrates my point nicely. The tax-deferred account is on the left, while the taxed annually (at only a 15% tax rate) is on the right.

Year	Uninterrupted	Taxed Annually
1	$2.00	$1.85
2	$4.00	$3.42
3	$8.00	$6.33
4	$16.00	$11.71
5	$32.00	$21.67
6	$64.00	$40.09
7	$128.00	$74.17
8	$256.00	$137.21
9	$512.00	$253.83
10	$1,024.00	$469.59
11	$2,048.00	$868.74
12	$4,096.00	$1,607.17
13	$8,192.00	$2,973.26
14	$16,384.00	$5,500.53
15	$32,768.00	$10,175.97
16	$65,536.00	$18,825.55
17	$131,072.00	$34,827.27
18	$262,144.00	$64,430.44
19	$524,288.00	$119,196.32
20	$1,048,576.00	$220,513.19

Of course, taxes will eventually be due when the funds are withdrawn from the account. But wouldn't you rather pay 15% taxes on $1,048,576 and net **$891,290 after tax**?

That's more than **$220,514**. I'd opt to pay taxes on four times as many gains every day of the week. Wouldn't you?

And most importantly, I hope you have seen that using Buffer annuities as part of your withdrawal or RMD strategy will make your money last longer (or leave a more significant legacy to family or the charities you care about) -- while taking market-induced stress away.

You'll sell and withdraw your stocks when they ended the previous year higher and not touch them (withdrawing funds from your Buffer annuity instead) when the markets closed the last year lower — selling high, not selling low.

This way, you let your stocks recover along with the market. It's not actually a loss until you take it (sell). That is why accountants call it "unrealized losses."

This strategy is the way to take as much of the sequence of returns risk off the table during your retirement. And as you'll recall, it is not the "average" return that you achieve in retirement; it is the sequence of those returns.

When your returns are excellent when beginning to take withdrawals from your account, the sequence of returns is your friend. However, the opposite is also true, and a "bad sequence" can ruin a retirement forever. This strategy significantly reduces that risk.

Although this book is about Buffer annuities, I'd be remiss not to even mention <u>guaranteed lifetime income</u> FIAs.

That type of annuity is <u>not</u> built for accumulation; it is designed to provide a guaranteed lifetime income for either a single life or a joint life (typically spouses).

Depending upon the product chosen, the guaranteed income could begin as early as immediately or perhaps eleven or more years out. The product may be designed for either a growing income or a fixed payment.

With products built for increasing income (usually tied to an inflation indicator (CPI), or based on how well the indexes perform, the guaranteed lifetime income usually starts at a lower level but can grow significantly.

In this case, your worst check… is your first check.

With a fixed lifetime income, the initial income is generally higher to begin with – but will <u>never</u> increase. You get no protection from inflation, which could be worrying if one or both spouses lives a long time in retirement.

Too often, people confuse this type of annuity with a SPIA (Single Premium Immediate Annuity). It's been a long time since I've recommended a SPIA since interest rates have been so very low for so long.

With a SPIA, you write a check to the insurance company. That money (100%) is now completely theirs. In return for that premium, they promise (and will) pay you a fixed sum every month for the rest of your life.

If you live a very long time, it may be a decent investment. If you pass away early, you'll never get your money back (nor will your heirs).

That type of SPIA (based on a single life) will provide you with the highest payment. If you want the income to cover two lives, the guaranteed payment will be lower. If you want your income payments to rise over time, the initial income would be even lower as well.

The guaranteed income would be even lower if you want to get a partial refund paid to your beneficiaries if you died before getting at least your initial premium back.

Again, with interest rates at historically low rates, it would have to be an exceptional circumstance for me to suggest buying a SPIA.

As an alternative to SPIAs, I like to use the guaranteed lifetime income annuities instead - where you do not give up total control of your assets. Should you die before the money is used, your beneficiaries would get any leftover funds in the account and sometimes much more.

With a SPIA, you can't change your mind after 10-30 days (depending on which state you live in). With my preferred income annuity products, you can usually take out 10% a year without any penalty, as with the Buffer annuities.

You can also get ALL of your money out by paying early surrender penalties. Not great, but it's better than having no access to your cash at all, like in the case of a SPIA.

The following chart shows what happens to your investment in a guaranteed income annuity (not a SPIA).

This client invested $150,000 (left axis), and we are planning to start taking the guaranteed income stream in the 12th year. You can see the line where the account is growing (I designed this particular annuity for maximum income and not for increasing the principal value).

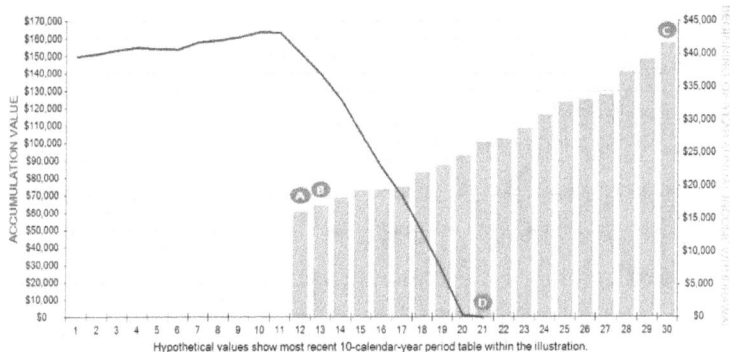

Hypothetical values show most recent 10-calendar-year period table within the illustration.

The blue bars represent the non-guaranteed income based on the returns of the last 10-year history of the indexes chosen. Their JOINT lifetime income is projected to start at about $16,000 per year and perhaps grow to over $40,000 per year by the 30th year (right axis).

It may not do that well since I don't think the next ten years will be as good as the last decade. But it may.

The guaranteed income (not shown) assumes his account earned 0% for thirty straight years. That's extremely unlikely – 0% returns for three decades. Wouldn't you say?

You can see the line (account value) eventually going down to zero in year 21. At that point, there's no money left in the account. No money left for any beneficiaries either.

But you can also see the <u>income continuing</u> – even after there is no money left in the account. Although the chart only goes for 30 years, the payments would never cease or stop increasing until <u>both</u> spouses had passed away.

Some of these annuities charge a fee for the guaranteed lifetime income, while others do not.

Annuities such as these provide another guaranteed monthly source of income – just like Social Security or a pension. Think of them as a private pension that you have much greater control over, than one from your employer or Social Security.

Some of these guaranteed income annuities also have some sort of "free" Long-Term Care (LTC) benefit. But beware, don't let some insurance agent try to "persuade" you that any such benefit is a true traditional LTC policy. You might get to use an extra "LTC benefit," but the moon and stars are going to have to align. But that's OK since you didn't pay a dime for that potential benefit either.

Let's get back to Buffer annuities.

In contrast with those guaranteed income annuities, Buffer annuities are built for maximum accumulation but have no attractive guaranteed income options. And as I've previously written, they are a near-perfect solution to the sequence of returns risk when taking RMDs or withdrawing funds for retirement income.

The two types of Fixed Indexed Annuities (FIAs) are two different financial tools – built for specific purposes. They are solutions for two separate concerns or problems.

Full disclosure: How do I get paid on Buffer annuities?

The insurance companies pay me 0.25% quarterly on your account balance annually to help you manage the annuity for as long as you keep the money in the account.

My 0.25% fee does NOT come out of/reduce your account balance. It does NOT lower your potential returns at all.

There are no sales loads (and no fees unless you opt to buy more options for potentially higher returns).

It is very much in our mutual interest to have your account grow (with or without the optional fees). I think you will want to keep going beyond the ten or 7-year holding period, and it's my job to make you very satisfied (and you can always take 10% out each year without any penalty).

But suppose something better comes along in the future. In that case, we can always move the account to something that better suits any new goals or changing circumstances after the initial holding period.

As a fee-based Certified Financial Planner™, I act as a Fiduciary whether I'm charging a fixed fee for a retirement income plan, managing assets at TD Ameritrade, Fidelity, or Schwab or recommending life insurance or annuities.

The CLIENT (under the Fiduciary standard) is at the center of all planning – not the PRODUCT (Suitability standard). I must always put the client's interest first and recommend what I would do if I had the same financial goals and were in the same situation. It's a good business practice too.

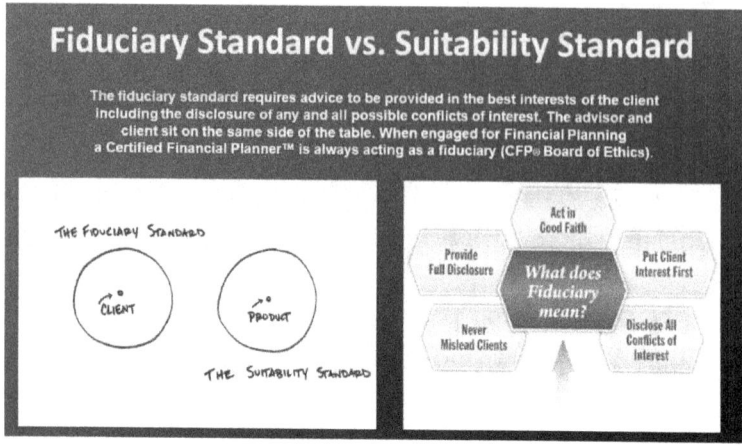

Again, these are not your ordinary fixed-indexed annuities. They are unique in their "safe accumulation" purpose and for use in a savvy RMD or withdrawal strategy. And as a Fiduciary, I'll let you know if a Buffer annuity makes sense for your personal situation and circumstances. But for the right goals, I believe they are diamonds in the rough.

I'll leave you with one more chart on the next page that I posted on Linked-In today. It's titled: "Is Targeting Yield/Dividends a Risky Strategy?"

It shows the drawdown (peak to trough losses) in various asset classes. Look at the bond categories and see what their historical maximum drawdown has been. Negative -12%, -17%, -30%, and -35%. Not typical, but they happen. Bonds aren't quite as safe as many folks believe they are. And check out the drawdowns of the equities! Peak to trough losses in various equity classes of up to 65%.

From 01/11/1973 to 10/3/1974, the S&P 500 had a whopping drawdown of -48.2%. From 11/28/1980 to 8/12/1982, the drawdown was "only" -27.1%. And from 8/25/1987 to 12/4/1987, the total drawdown was -33.5%.

More recently, from 3/24/2000 to 10/9/2002, the S&P 500 had a huge drawdown of -49.1%. From 10/9/2007 to 3/9/2009, the S&P 500 had a massive drawdown of -56.8%. And the short-lived COVID crash from 2/19/2020 to 3/23/2020, a loss of -33.9% in the index.

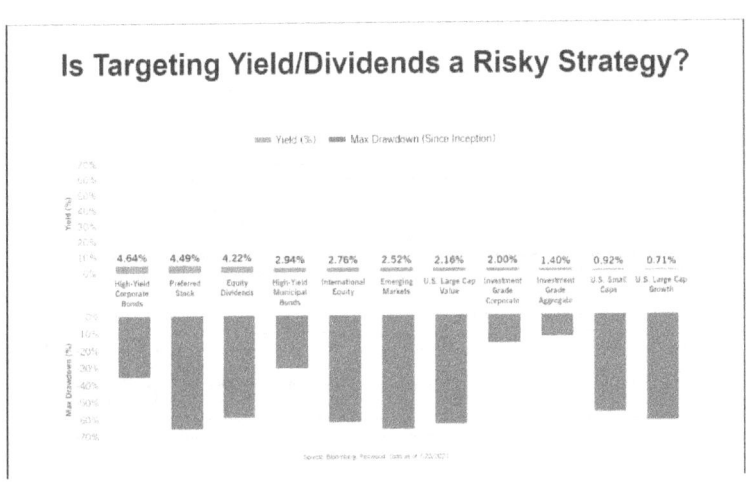

So again, Buffer annuities can never suffer market losses. No market-based drawdowns. ZERO is your HERO.

For a 60% stock and 40% bond portfolio, bond drawdowns can occur at the same time that equities are tanking.

The smart RMD or income withdrawal strategy described in this book can help you from "selling low" and allow your investments to recover – as markets always have.

And the past "NET" returns (even after paying a fee for more upside) of 5%, 6%, or even higher aren't too shabby. I genuinely expect Buffer annuities to outperform bonds.

If you have an interest in exploring this potential option as a bond (or stock) alternative for a traditional IRA or ROTH, 401K rollover, or a taxable brokerage account, please contact me for more details.

We would look at how this type of product may make sense for yourself or someone you care about, (such as a parent or sibling) as part of a withdrawal plan.

Of course, there will be no obligation, cost, or hassle. I've been a professional fee-based planner for over 20 years – not a starving insurance agent. There's no cost to you to investigate these or any of my financial services further.

I am licensed in most states for insurance and nearly every state as an Investment Advisor Representative with other non-traditional "bond-alternative" and equity strategies for investors who want higher returns with less risk. We also offer research-driven, non-cookie cutter investment portfolios to limit drawdown in both equities and bonds.

I look forward to the opportunity to discuss how any of my professional services can improve your financial future.

About the Author: Mark J. Orr, CFP® RICP®
PROACTIVE Tax Planning, LLC
www.SmartFinancialPlanning.com
770-777-8309 Office
mark@SmartFinancialPlanning.com

Mark has been a practicing Certified Financial Planner™ since 2000. Certified Financial Planners are held to the strictest ethical and fiduciary standards. He has also earned the year-long Retirement Income Certified Professional® (RICP®) designation. Since 1997, he has held life, health, and the Series 7 Securities license (no longer maintained) and became a Registered Investment Advisor soon after owning his own fee-based firm from 1999-2016.

He is now an Investment Advisor Representative with Retirement Wealth Advisors (RWA), where he manages his clients' stock and bond market-based investments – applying tactical money management mainly using index ETFs. These fee-only accounts are allocated into portfolios based on a client's risk tolerance, tax situation, time horizon, and income and legacy goals. Mark always acts in his role as a Fiduciary.

Our first focus is on reducing the sequence of returns risk (and drawdown) while capturing as much of the market's upside as possible with the daily oversight from our full-time professional investment committee.

He is also the author of three other books: 1) "Social Security Income Planning: The Baby Boomers' 2022 Guide to Maximize Your Retirement Benefits" 2) "Retirement Income Planning" 3) "Get Me to Zero: Use the 2022 Tax Code to Pay as Little as ZERO taxes During Retirement" (which includes much of this book fully describing the TRIPLE ZERO™ plan as one of the seven tax-free planning strategies).

He has led dozens of public seminars on various financial planning and retirement topics. He's been quoted twice in both the USA TODAY and cnbc.com, as well as being a guest on several morning radio shows across the country.

Prior to the financial services business, Mark spent the early part of his career in the luxury resort real estate development and marketing industry – managing $100 million of sales in Europe over a 7-year period. That was back when that was "real" money -- lol! After that, he owned a few franchises and then sold those businesses.

He is a four-time past board member of his Rotary Club and continues to be active in community service through the Rotary Club. On a personal note, Mark and Norma live in Alpharetta, Georgia, and love to travel – especially to warm sandy beaches. Staying in good shape is very important to him and he enjoys excellent red wine.

Finally, he is the very proud father of three grown children (Megan, Marina, and Michael) and two wonderful grandchildren.

Acknowledgments and Disclosures

The opinions and views written in this book are those of the author and do not necessarily represent those of any person, organization, or firm that I have been associated with (either in the past, are currently, or may be in the future). This book is intended to provide general information only and that no individual professional financial advice is offered herein. The author is not a CPA or certified tax professional. The author is not an attorney.

Neither the author nor publisher intend to or is rendering any professional services including but not limited to: tax advice, investment advice, insurance advice, legal advice, or mortgage advice. This book, nor any words written within its pages should be interpreted as giving any such personal/individual advice and should not be relied upon.

Any mention of financial products, investment managers, investment advisory services, etc., should not be construed as an offer to buy, sell or exchange any financial product or service.

The author and publisher disclaim any responsibility for any reader taking any liability, or loss incurred as a consequence of any implementation (or even non-implementation) on the information provided herein. No book intended as general information and sold to the general public can be construed to offer specific and personal financial, investment, insurance, tax, or legal advice.

All readers who require personal advice and professional financial service should seek an experienced, qualified, and appropriately licensed advisor (relevant to such advice) and not solely rely on the contents of this or any book to make any personal financial decision.

Insurance products are not investments. All insurance products are backed based solely on the financial strength and the claims-paying ability of the insurer which issues the policy or contract. Use of the terms "Principal Protected," "Guaranteed," "Safe," "Secure," and any and all such similar words when describing any insurance product are based entirely on the fact of contractual guarantees which rely on the financial strength and claims-paying ability of the insurance company.

Fixed Indexed Annuity (FIA) and IUL insurance policies are not stock, bond, or investments and have no direct participation in the stock or bond markets. You are not buying any bonds, shares of stocks, or shares in an index, nor do they include dividends or interest of any stock, bond, or market index.

Investment Advisory Services are offered through Retirement Wealth Advisors (RWA), an SEC Registered Investment Advisor. Mark J. Orr and RWA are not affiliated. Investing involves risk, including the potential loss of principal. No investment strategy can guarantee a profit or protect against loss in periods of declining values. Opinions expressed are subject to change without notice and are not intended as investment advice or to predict future performance.

Past performance does not guarantee future results. Consult your financial professional before making any investment decision. All life insurance, fixed annuity products, fees for retirement income plans, and advanced income tax planning for business owners are sold separately through Mark J. ORR, CFP®/PROACTIVE Tax Planning LLC.

For more information on Fixed Indexed Annuities and Retirement Income Planning strategies, get my book:

"[Retirement Income Planning](#)" at amazon

www.ingramcontent.com/pod-product-compliance
Lightning Source LLC
Chambersburg PA
CBHW052332220526
45472CB00001B/385